EQUALITY ISSUES
IN PRIMARY SCHOOLS

JOHN BOYD

P·C·P
Paul Chapman
Publishing Ltd

Copyright © 1989 John Boyd

First published 1989

Paul Chapman Publishing Ltd
144 Liverpool Road
London N1 1LA

British Library Cataloguing in Publication Data

Boyd, John, *1935–*
    Equality issues in primary schools.
    1. Great Britain. Primary schools. Students.
    Education. Equality of opportunity
    I. Title
    372.18

ISBN 1–85396–038–1

Typeset by Inforum Typesetting, Portsmouth
Printed and bound in Great Britain by
Butler & Tanner Ltd, Frome and London

To Beryl, Karen and Cathryn

CONTENTS

INTRODUCTION

Equality in terms of equal opportunities in an educational context is as old as the century: it dates from the point when mass education beyond that provided in elementary schools was first recognized as a possibility. The notion of the 'ladder of opportunity', whereby bright children from top elementary classes could gain access by a scholarship to the new, county secondary schools established by the 1902 Act, was an acknowledgement that it was not only possible to be working class and talented, but also that the State education system should be a means by which such gifts should be developed. Thus, the notion – which is meritocratic rather than egalitarian – had a class focus that dominated until the 1970s. Characteristic research in the 1950s and 1960s focused on social-class influences on educability and the self-fulfilling prophecies established by streaming and secondary-school selection, and the wastage of working-class talent that resulted from how these operated. For primary education, the Plowden Report was official recognition of the claimed effects of material and 'cultural' deprivation on working-class children's performance.

By the mid-1970s, the focus of the debate had shifted to race and gender, highlighted by legislation that was concerned with discriminatory practices in employment and housing – the Sex Discrimination Act of 1975, and the Race Relations Act in 1976. Both Acts included educational references that have not so far been applied to the problems of unequal treatment and performance in schools. The Warnock Committee's recommendation that disabled children should be integrated into mainstream education broadened this new focus, but race and, to a lesser extent, gender, are still the dominant issues.

Unlike the earlier conception of inequality with its class basis, the new race-and-gender formulation has fuelled a campaign: many local authorities in England and Wales now proclaim themselves in posts advertisements as equal opportunities' employers, and about half have produced equality statements and guidelines for their schools to follow when formulating their own responses and making the necessary curricular and resource changes. Consequently, a large number of teachers will be acquainted with the issues and their educational implications to varying degrees depending on their local authority's ideological viewpoint and implementation approach.

The purpose of this book is essentially practical: to develop a critical and practical framework for primary teachers to plan and implement school-based equality policies. Such policy-making is unlike the more technical demands made on teachers by conventional innovation such as introducing new teaching of reading or mathematics materials. Curricular and resources changes of this kind are often generated within the school itself, frequently resulting from internal appraisal and review. Teachers, of course, have to be convinced of the rightness of a proposed innovation – it has to accord with their own beliefs about teaching and learning, and be a clear improvement on what it is intended to replace. After this, it will draw on teachers' experience and expertise by posing essentially technical problems concerning teaching methods and the use of new resources. Such change is stressful because teachers for a period are deskilled while they come to terms with the new order; this temporary incompetence threatens such crucial factors as class control. Most curricular innovations are clearly educational and practical in their implications because they have no other purpose than to improve the quality of learning in a curricular area. More radical changes such as abolishing reading schemes and adopting a 'real-books' approach in teaching reading will be more likely to challenge teachers ideologically.

In this, they begin to resemble equality policy-making. Since the concept of equality is political and ethical before it is educational, such policies can confront teachers with personal and professional value-conflicts, particularly for those who are unsure of or disagree with the local authority's viewpoint. At an extreme, some county-hall ideologies may be seen by teachers as attempted indoctrination, in which they are used as agents of social engineering. Or the policy might be judged as irrelevant in a school where teachers assert that there are no problems. There is a broad continuum of viewpoints. To illustrate this, Arnot (1985) has drawn attention to the opposed ideological positions resulting from applying a Crosland-type 'weak' or 'strong' interpretation to sex equality. The 'weak' interpretation claims that equality is attained when boys and girls have equal access to education, but the 'strong' viewpoint argues that this is not enough. Access is only the first step towards real equality, which is the equal opportunity to achieve in education, and which entails some form of positive discrimination. These interpretations divide what she describes as the 'egalitarians' from the 'feminists' in the pursuit of sex equality.

The issues of sexism and racism figure in different ways in most viewpoints. For example, what can be described generically as schooling for gender or racial equality can be differentiated in radical or liberal terms according to how they interpret sexism and racism. Thus, the radical view is represented by anti-sexism and anti-racism, and the liberal by sex equity and multiculturalism. The more extreme version of anti-sexism/racism takes the view that sexism and racism are endemic in society, in both personal/psychological and structural forms. The implication is that social institutions like schools are inherently sexist and racist in operation and that changes in the political and social structure will be needed to eradicate this. A more moderate version of anti-sexism/racism, as that adopted by local authorities such as Berkshire and ILEA, stops short of advocating structural change but argues that sexism and racism are social and structural evils to be confronted by and through individual initiatives and legislation. The liberal sex-equity and multicultural positions acknowledge personal and, to a lesser extent, structural sexism and racism as influences on school achievement and seek change through modifying the curriculum, resources and organization of schools. The problem of interpretation and the value-conflicts it can cause is intensified by the centralist top-down style of innovation adopted by local authorities such as ILEA, Brent and Haringey, in which the official county-hall standpoint on equality in relation to class, race and gender is not perceived by teachers as being open to negotiation.

Primary schools are focused on because of their strong socialization role, coupled with evidence from research that suggests that race and gender identification and stereotyping are well established in children by the time they start school. If some of these negative effects of early socialization are to be counteracted in schools, there is a need for all learning experiences in primary classrooms to be founded on a considered and assimilated equality stance. The basic conditions for achieving this inhere in child-centredness, the dominant ideology of British primary education, with its central principle of respect for all children as individual learners. It is a truism to claim that every initial primary-teacher education course in Britain is child-centred in its aims and objectives; likewise every local authority subscribes to child-centredness in some form as its official stance on primary teaching and learning. At the same time, only a small proportion of primary teachers are child-centred in their approaches and this has not changed much in the twenty years following Plowden. If this is so, how can child-centredness be a satisfactory basis for developing equality?

The problems with traditional child-centredness, especially from a new teacher's viewpoint, are those of misunderstanding and misapplication. Various conflicting messages can be transmitted at the initial teacher-education stage. For example, an over-simple understanding of Piaget can result in his stages being applied rigidly so that the orthodoxy of stage-compartmentalization in learning replaces the subject-compartments ortho-doxy rejected by child-centredness. The claims for experiential and discovery-learning will be finely balanced against the new teacher's concern to maintain order. Starting from where the children are can be very difficult in classes where there is a wide ability range. At the same time, as with all ideologies, child-centredness is prescriptive: it prescribes certain teaching and learning approaches based on an account of the nature of childhood that conflates individual and educational development. This implies that children will prosper educationally in a learning environment in which they can pursue their own interests. Overarching this is the belief in childhood innocence, or that while children's behaviour might be objectionable, it is never malicious. In summary, unassimilated child-centredness, instead of being understood as a philosophy of learning and teaching, can be taken to be a set of practical guidelines that, when tested, are found to work only with small groups of children, or not at all. For it to become a workable professional ideology, it has to be individually reinterpreted and recon-structed by each primary teacher.

Its traditional imperatives point to an education to be conducted in seclusion, almost as if the world outside childhood is taken to be as corrupt as Rousseau believed it to be. Further, while development is taken to be 'natural', some of its more negative manifestations, for example, in the form of embryonic race and sex prejudices are taken to be unnatural and brought about by conditions outside the school. It follows that the best conditions for fostering natural individual development will be in classrooms with carefully-controlled learning environments. Hence the tendency to perceive learning as necessarily taking place in a social vacuum. But if the concern really is for the 'whole child', the social dimension cannot be denied. The unreality of the position is intensified by the fact that children only spend about one-fifth of the week in school, and presumably for the rest of the time when they are not sleeping are members of society.

It is argued that if child-centredness is reconceptualized so that the social is held to be as important as the individual dimension, it could rightly claim to be concerned with childhood as a whole; it would be a less exclusive account of the conditions necessary to development and learning and would therefore provide a sounder basis on which teachers might develop their own professional ideologies. In turn, this is crucial for developing a commitment to the principle of equality in children's learning experiences since it would emphasize children's membership of a society and the need for them to be critically aware of its dominant beliefs and values.

If schools are to develop effective policies, independently or within local-authority guidelines, teachers and other adults in a school will need to be able to debate and to resolve value issues and develop practices that are workable on their terms. Unless there is openness, individual dissent will be masked in the production of a policy that only superficially represents consensus. It is likely to gather dust on a staffroom shelf, which is only shaken off when the adviser visits. In the relative privacy of their own classrooms, teachers will filter local-authority ideology through their own value systems. What they implement will be what they understand and agree with. All change involves risk-taking; change that might also challenge strong political and social beliefs will be even more hazardous. Because of the requirement to act, and perhaps because individual teachers can feel themselves to be relatively powerless in the face of local-authority ideologies, it is possible that they will submerge their differences in order to produce the policy. But a policy formulated in a spirit of *fait accompli*, or under duress, will hardly be operable.

It is crucial to the production of a workable and authoritative policy that teachers have a full opportunity to debate and to resolve value-conflicts based on as complete an understanding as possible of the complexities involved. A central issue will be the nature of equality itself as a principle informing practice, the various ideological interpretations made of it and their practical implications in and beyond school. The key to understanding what equality means lies in its inherently practical nature: as a major moral principle it necessarily commits people to act in situations in which they perceive there is unfairness, discrimination and wasted talents. How they respond will depend as much on emotions such as compassion as on logic and rational enquiry.

Part of what is entailed in developing a critical framework for policy-making depends on teachers' drawing upon the appropriate bodies of knowledge, research evidence and academic discourse in order to provide themselves with a firm justification for their decisions. If a reasoned, justifiable basis for change is to be established, it is important that teachers do have access to relevant research findings and commentaries. There is a difference between this material, which would include action research accounts and case-studies of attempted equal-opportunities policies implementation, together with curricular and organizational change, and what might be termed traditional educational theory, with its roots in disciplines such as history, philosophy, psychology and sociology. The theory–practice relationship can be improved by making the practices of classroom and school life the subject of study, so that data from teachers' observations of the processes operating in their own classrooms can be used to make practical decisions. ILEA's anti-sexism policy recommends this approach as a basis for teachers' self-informing and decision-making. To take an example, an infants' teacher who observes that the home corner is monopolized by girls and the Lego by boys will not necessarily be seeing anything new, but she is more likely to be aware of the need to modify this situation if her observations are carried out in the process of developing an equality policy. She will be in an even better position to initiate change if she is also acquainted with some of the research into the socially-learned interests and activities of boys and girls. Small-scale participant and non-participant observation studies of the type now commonly undertaken by teacher-students on in-service bachelor of education and diploma course are a usable model for investigating the process of curricular and organizational change. So too is the classroom-based Ford T Project's approach with its triangulation method in which the observational accounts of teachers, pupils and observers are used to identify the principles underpinning decision-making. The atheoretical stance of many teachers can be countered by putting them in touch with research material that is concerned with classroom conditions. At the same time, teaching as an activity is not exempt from the need for it to be guided, explained and justified, and teachers need both to generate and to draw upon theories that can do this if they are to develop a clearer understanding of the processes at work in their classrooms.

It is argued that a school staff – teachers and ancillary workers – needs to debate and to resolve values and practices issues as a condition for implementing workable policies. But there is a conflict between giving schools the necessary responsibility and autonomy to do this and the top-down innovation strategies utilized by some local authorities. The dilemma is that if a strong central control is exercised, in which much of the policy decision-making responsibility is taken by the local authority, teachers will claim that their professional judgement as to what is right and wrong for their children is pre-empted. But, if more power is given to the schools, their responses may differ from the county-hall line. Schools with a long history of developing multicultural or anti-racist strategies, for example, may acknowledge an authority's right to define the problem but not necessarily its solution. What this suggests is that some equalization of power and responsibility will enable an authority's policy to be implemented according to differing needs and situations.

Much of this suggests the inherent school and classroom-based nature of innovation; this is a truism in the sense that it works to the extent that teachers implement it. But this is not to claim that teachers should be the sole arbiters of change, and there is some research evidence suggesting that primary teachers understand the shared nature of this responsibility.

A positive climate for change will be generated in a school by such qualities as effective, consultative leadership, recognition of professional expertise between peers and by the head, and effective resourcing, including adequate time to evaluate proposals. Hidden curricular factors such as high morale, group cohesion and sufficient institutional self-confidence to be able to call in experts as consultants are indicators of such a climate. The concept of collegiality in which a group of professionals works to achieve agreed goals by allocating responsibilities according to the knowledge and expertise of individual members is an effective referential framework for school-based innovation. So far as equality policy-based innovation is concerned, planned change needs to include the ancillary workers alongside the teachers since good classroom practice can be cancelled out by insensitive or prejudiced actions in the playground or the meals queue.

The proposed model for equal-opportunities school-based innovation takes account of teacher, ancillary worker, school and local-authority factors. It functions in three stages: first, debates over values, beliefs and differing interpretations have to be settled between teacher and non-teaching colleagues. It hardly needs to be said that this experience can often be challenging; indeed traumatic. Second, a policy is formulated based on an agreed position. Third, the policy is implemented through curricular and resource renewal and innovation, and organizational changes. At the third stage, teachers' technical expertise comes into its own once the values position is resolved, or where at least there is a consensus view on how to proceed. What is important is that a rational conceptual framework for necessary change is developed so that a concern for equality becomes part of the normal experience of teaching and learning.

1
PRIMARY EDUCATION AND CHILD-CENTREDNESS

This chapter begins with a critique of the main principles and practices of child-centredness – the dominant ideology of primary education in Britain – in order to redevelop it so that its social dimension is as important as its concern for individuality. This has two purposes: to provide teachers with reference points for developing their own ideologies of primary practice, and to develop a facilitating framework for implementing equal opportunities in schools and classrooms. A related major concern here is the meritocratic effects of the narrow definition of achievement that prevails in the education system; if it can be redefined so that it includes practical, personal and collaborative achievements, the charge of meritocracy can be countered and a better basis for implementing equal opportunities established.

Origins and Basis of Child-Centredness

The history of child-centredness is almost synonymous with that of primary education. It has attained a degree of authority such that it tends to be regarded by educationalists as a substantiated body of knowledge, integrating such key factors as the nature of childhood, aspects of human development, the organization of learning and teaching and curriculum planning. Alexander (1984; in Carrington and Short, 1987, p. 5) argues that the main claims of child-centredness are as follows:

(1) psychological and social development passes through a number of pre-set 'stages' which, in turn, determine children's 'readiness' (viz., capacity) to handle different types of cognitive task, (sequential developmentalism);

(2) teachers should respond to children as unique individuals;
(3) play is the principal means of learning in early childhood;
(4) young children, while capable of unacceptable behaviour, are nevertheless free from malicious intent.

As a conceptual framework informing practice, its roots are in materialist philosophy: knowledge is acquired through an individual's experience of the world, in contrast to the rationalist epistemology, in which knowledge exists independently of the knower. It follows that knowledge is acquired through the individual's direct and active engagement with the material world, and that the teacher's role is to provide an environment rich in potential learning possibilities. The writings of educationalists and philosophers such as Locke, Rousseau and Froebel, through to Dewey and Bruner emphasize that the process by which human beings achieve knowledge and become educated is essentially experiential.

Briefly, the rationalist account of knowledge maintains that information derived from sense experience is false knowledge, since the material world is constantly changing. The supreme model of rational – that is, logical, deductive knowledge – is mathematics: two plus two equals four is permanent and unchanging and does not have to be demonstrated and proven over and over again. Plato, the supreme rationalist, went so far as to claim that only mathematics and logic were certain forms of knowledge. The empiricist account takes the opposing view, that knowledge is derived from sense impressions gained by experience and observation. In Locke's account, the human mind at birth is a *tabula rasa* or blank slate: experience is the means by which knowledge is printed on it. Because experience differs between individuals, human knowledge can only be probable, but this provisional knowledge is more valuable than the alleged certain knowledge of the rationalists because it is more usable.

These views still influence teaching and learning and the ways in which curricular knowledge is seen; despite their apparent remoteness from practical matters, two clear-cut viewpoints have developed from them that figure, for example, in studies of teacher and pupil style such as ORACLE, Barnes' (1976) definitions of transmissive and interpretative teaching, Stenhouse's (1975) advocacy of processes-based curriculum planning rather than objectives to be attained, and Hirst's (1974) claim that human knowledge is divided into a fixed number of forms. Put simply, in the rationalist account, knowledge is unchanging, independent of human minds. The teacher's task is to initiate pupils into traditionally-valued propositional knowledge in the form of abstract disciplines, mathematics being the chief one. Thus, a curriculum divided into subjects is a reflection of the rationalist account since it carries the assumption that knowledge by its nature is categorized into a number of discrete areas. Teachers are characterized as subject experts with pupils as potential acquirers of their knowledge. In the empiricist account, knowledge is generated by the activity of individual minds and is therefore provisional and changing. It follows that laws and concepts are not handed down but are formulated as explanations of the workings of the physical world. For teachers, this places the emphasis on the learner's experiences, interpretations and hypotheses since knowledge is by its nature personally acquired. Consequently, a subject-based curriculum is in conflict with this view of knowledge because it assumes a permanency that does not exist. The distinction between teachers and learners is blurred since teachers are not curriculum experts but arrangers and facilitators of knowledge development through the learning environments for which they are responsible. Again, simply, the rationalist approach is like traditional secondary education in being curriculum and knowledge-centred, while the empiricist approach with its emphasis on the individual's construction of knowledge in an undifferentiated-curriculum framework is primary and child-centred.

As an ideology of schooling, child-centredness was a reaction against the authoritarian ethos, narrow skills-based curriculum and social-control emphasis of the nineteenth-century elementary schools in Britain and the USA on the part of educators concerned with early childhood education. Its focal point was a rediscovered concern for the nature and value of childhood, following Rousseau and Froebel a hundred years earlier. In Britain, it also coincided with the growth of compulsory elementary schooling following the Education Act 1870 by which the new School Boards could require children to attend for set periods of time, though with provisions for part-time schooling where children were needed as factory or agricultural workers. An Act in 1880 brought in compulsion on a national basis. Important at this time was a decline in the use of child labour in industry, through the cumulative effects of the Factory Acts and also for reasons of economic efficiency: technology was advancing to the point where skilled adult operators rather than children were needed. It is significant also that the early nineteenth-century Froebellian notion of play was rediscovered at this time when urban child labour was in decline and increasingly socially disapproved of. The elementary schools had defined the nature of childhood in terms of pupildom; it was for the new progressives to redevelop childhood beyond the social-utility terms of reference determined by the elementary schools. The Froebellian slogan, 'play is the work of the child', has therefore more than an educational resonance.

Child-centredness can also be seen as a teacher's status enhancer. Alexander (1984) argues that one of the reasons why it came into prominence when it did was to justify class teaching as the agreed universal form for organizing teachers and children in elementary and, later, in primary schools. As the rationale for a pedagogy, it provided increasingly-professionalized teachers with a specialized body of knowledge to reinforce their new professional identities. The marginal status, first of elementary and then of primary teachers as semi- or minor professionals, made the articulation of an organizing ideology drawing on high-status knowledge the more important as a status-improving replacement of the 'missionary ideology' of elementary teachers, in Grace's (1978) terms.

It was accepted as the official Board of Education ideology. The beginnings of this are detectable in the 1904 *Elementary Code*, the 1905 *Handbook of Suggestions* for elementary school-teachers and in an oppositional context in Edmund Holmes' (1911) *What Is and What Might Be*. Selleck (1972) reveals that progressive child-centred methods were being used in Britain from the early nineteenth century by a number of elementary teachers. 'Pure' child-centredness, or education as personal and individual development, was very much seen as the appropriate basis for educating primary-age children, but a different rationale began to be applied when the question of whether State education should go beyond primary provision began to be raised. The plea for a limited amount and form of social justice couched in equality-of-opportunity terms was behind the idea that schooling should be a number of stages of sequential development rather than a single complete experience. From the 1920s, this and other influential ideas informed educational policy on State schooling. In some ways they reinforced and in others they conflicted with its class-structure basis of provision, in the hands of policy-producing committees. Thus, the dominant claim that intelligence was genetically inherited, sharpened by the possibility of predicting attainment by using intelligence tests, tended to confirm what had always been believed – that only a small proportion of working-class children would benefit from a post-elementary academic education. The 1926 Hadow Report is characteristic: it sought to abolish the mass-education elementary system by recommending a sequential primary–secondary system but retained its class basis through the provision of three levels of secondary education in grammar, secondary-technical and secondary-modern schools. The 1938 Spens and 1943 Norwood Reports are harder-line statements of this position, with Norwood actually proposing and describing in some detail three kinds of secondary pupils to fit the schools provided. So, what appeared to be progressive, with different kinds of schools having parity of esteem and offering different educational experiences to children according to their aptitudes and interests, in reality conformed with the class structure of British society with its built-in assumptions about class-based levels of educability. There can only be a residual child-centredness in the notion that children will develop in an educational setting that accords with their potential when this is set in the context of a stratified society; the essential individualistic rationale of the ideology is submerged by all three reports' categorization of pupils to fit different kinds of schools that culminates in Norwood's three types. The Education Act 1944 as the political projection of this thinking, likewise expressed the rhetoric of child-centredness in its requirement that children should be educated according to their age, ability and aptitude, but the reality was that these were defined in terms of the assumed superiority of traditional academic education over other types.

The consequence of separating the system into primary and secondary stages was that of separate development, with only the mechanism of secondary selection connecting them. The usual practice of separation into infant and junior schools and departments created another division in which infant schools developed a distinctive and well-articulated child-centred ethic. Junior schools arguably did not achieve this kind of identity, partly because of their necessary preoccupation with the eleven-plus and the pressure to get as many children as possible into grammar schools.

Campbell (1985, p. 150) describes the post-1944 development of the official ideology in terms of three iconographies: 'Images of this kind serve to portray in vivid, condensed and potent form the values that schools should adhere to, rather as icons in Eastern Orthodox churches help worshippers to concentrate their devotion on the central figures of their belief system'. The 'humane meritocratic' style of the 1950s sponsored academic merit through setting and streaming but not at the expense of giving less-able children a sense of failure, since affective goals in the form of personality development were also acknowledged. The 'emotional integrative' style of the 1960s, most fully expressed in Plowden, is the most-clearly child-centred, while the 1970s 'community oriented' transformed social pathology-inspired views of deprivation into community-related strengths respecting cultural diversity. The *Educational Priority* series of reports in the early 1970s and the writings of Midwinter (for example, 1972, 1973) typify this icon.

Child-Centredness and Curriculum Planning

To continue the analogy, the 1980s can be described as 'curriculum oriented' with its roots in the 1960s. Plowden demonstrated the stress caused by trying to locate child-centredness in an essentialist-curriculum framework, by emphasizing children's individual development, the 'hovering-provider' role of the teacher and socially-influenced definitions of educability, but retaining a highly-traditional, subject-based account of the primary curriculum. The HMI survey, *Primary Education in England* (DES, 1978), in taking stock of Plowden advances, was strongly curriculum focused, while all the DES and HMI discussion and policy formation papers from *Curriculum 11–16* in 1977 have been centrally concerned with defining the curriculum for State primary and secondary schools, a process that reached its culmination with the Education Act 1988. This curriculum orientation can be traced back to the essentialist curriculum of the *Revised Code* and the *Elementary Codes* published yearly that first prescribed, and from 1904 advised teachers, what elementary school-children should be taught. The traditional subject emphasis of DES curricular pronouncements, which contrast with the more-liberal thinking of HMI, represent in Alexander's (1984) terms a society-centred view – an updated social-utility curriculum allied to a performance-objectives programme for pupil assessment. In some contrast, and isolation, the last working paper of the abolished Schools Council, *Primary Practice* (1983), is a present- and future-oriented statement in which the tenets of child-centredness are incorporated in a curriculum that engages issues directly affecting children's lives inside and outside schools and classrooms. Arguably, it is the only coherent statement on primary education that integrates child-centredness and curriculum planning in a way that respects children's everyday knowledge and concerns and avoids the Deweyan charge of child–curriculum polarity.

In considering further the linkages and disjunctions between child-centredness and curriculum planning, the four ideologies suggested by Richards (1982) are relevant as focal points of conflict throughout the 1970s and continuing into the 1980s: with the central government implementation of a common curriculum the tensions become even more acute especially where innovation, at all levels, is concerned. Liberal romanticism emphasizes the child in an experiental-learning setting, while the other three are identified by their different quasi-political stances – educational conservatism stresses traditional skills and a subject-based curriculum, while liberal conservatism, a compromise position, locates children's learning in their own experiences but allows curriculum planning by teachers. Social democracy, the most relevant here, considers the curriculum as a means by which social-justice goals might be achieved. All are mentioned here because all still function in the late 1980s – sometimes in the same school! They typify in different ways the increasing curriculum orientation of primary schooling, underpinned by major modifications in primary-teacher education brought about by the subject-study clauses in the DES Circular 3/84, which now affect all initial teacher-education courses. This emphasis on the curriculum and curriculum planning signals a move away from the canons of child-centredness that were the basis of teacher-education courses from the 1960s onward.

Critics of Child-Centredness

Criticisms of child-centredness since Plowden have been educational, political and derived from empirical research evidence. The educationalists were led by R.S. Peters and R.F. Dearden (for example, see Peters, 1969) who attacked the report and, by implication, child-centredness in theory and practice, for its sketchy treatment of aims and its lack of analysis of children's needs and interests as the mainsprings of learning. Dearden especially (1968) criticized the ways in which so-called evidence from child-development studies was co-opted to make links between children's growth and maturation and their educational needs and interests, as the means by which enquiry-based learning could be justified. The political critics were from the Right and the Left – the first represented by the *Black Paper* authors (for example, Cox and Dyson, 1969), who linked progressive child-centred practices with low standards of basic-skills attainment, poor preparation for subjects-based secondary schooling and inadequate social training. The second were characterized by Marxist educationists such as Sharp and Green (1975), who argued that the progressive ideology did not take account, except through a deficit explanation, of structural inequalities in society leading to an unequal distribution of rewards and prestige. Empirical studies on teaching and learning styles such as Bennett's (1976) and ORACLE, reinforced by two HMI surveys, have been arguably more influential in leading both teacher and public opinion, with the Bennett and ORACLE work receiving full media treatment in their days. Both studies raised questions about the effectiveness of child-centred approaches; ORACLE extended this debate by considering the effects of several different kinds of teaching style on children's attainments. Also, so far as curriculum commonality is concerned, ORACLE revealed a teacher-defined curriculum that operated across the range of styles in which language and mathematics occupied up to two-thirds of the learning time available.

Both the Bennett and ORACLE studies concerned junior and not infant teachers. Some research evidence suggests (for example, Ashton, Kneen and Davies, 1975) that only a small proportion of junior teachers are 'individualistic', or child-centred in their beliefs and practices, compared with King (1978) who suggests that infant teachers widely accept the main traditional imperatives of child-centredness. This position might be changing, due to the practice of amalgamating separate infant and junior schools into primary schools catering for the 5–11-years age-group. But it is clear from this range of evidence that while child-centredness remains the dominant official ideology of primary education – since Plowden – the proportion of teachers who practise it has changed little in twenty years.

Child-Centredness and Social Justice

At face value there is congruence between child-centredness and social justice. The first emphasizes individual children's growth and development in a beneficial educational climate, with the aim of personal autonomy being achieved in adulthood. The second also emphasizes individual action through the promotion of rational and responsible attitudes towards moral responsibility. These points suggest that the values of a democratically-ordered society, for instance, are reflected in child-centredness. But further analysis suggests there are conflicts between its traditional precepts and school practices that make this connection less tenable.

First, there is conflict between the declared aims of progressive child-centred education and the socialization function of schools, especially in State-maintained education systems. At the curricular level, there is tension between the principle of starting from where the child is, which requires that knowledge is attained through individuals' exploring their environments and formulating their own explanations for what they perceive, and curriculum planning in the sense of operating a pre-arranged curriculum, as argued for example in Boyd (1984). At this level, conflict is emphasized by the requirement that State schools adhere to an essentialist view of school knowledge, not determined by them, which requires that individuals are initiated into a body of knowledge that incorporates what are held to be the essential skills, values, attitudes and modes of thought required for viable adulthood in this society. Of course, a State-defined common curriculum is a natural development of this position. Since the so-called Great Debate in 1976, the DES and the HMI – through a series of policy-formation and discussion papers (for example, DES, 1977, 1980, 1981, 1985a, 1987) – have identified a common curriculum that could not be implemented directly without legislation and that the DES tried to implement indirectly through the curricular guidelines local authorities were required to produce for schools' use as a result of the Circular 14/77 review.

Second, at the level of pedagogy and organization, a majority of teachers continue to maintain through their choice of methods, as evidenced in ORACLE, that child-centred education cannot be successfully practised, especially with large classes. For teachers in inner-city schools, the claim is strengthened by the actual and apparent difficulties of maintaining learning with strongly-heterogeneous intakes often also suffering from economic deprivation. These conflicts convey a strong sense of decisions being made outside schools that reduce teachers' spheres of responsibility; they are likely to affect how teachers judge the relevance or possibility of promoting equality, whether through school policies or as class teachers. Being child-centred 'goes with' promoting equality at the values level, but does this still apply when practical compromises have to be made? What seems to be at issue is the exclusive nature of traditional child-centredness – specifically, its lack of a developed social dimension. For example, King's (1978) observational study of infant teachers indicates that such principles as sequential developmentalism, individualism, the value of play in promoting learning and childhood innocence are widely accepted by them as the basis of their professional practice. A different approach that illustrates this sense of the child in a social vacuum in child-centredness was adopted by the Schools Council Aims of Primary Education Project in the 1970s. It distinguished between 'societal' and 'individualistic' teachers. 'Societal' broadly corresponds with informal or transmissive approaches:

> They most want children to read fluently, accurately and with understanding. They want them to write clear and meaningful, grammatical, correctly spelt English in legible handwriting. They want children to be able to do arithmetical computations and to cope with the mathematics of everyday situations. . . . Within this same group of aims comes the desire for children to be obedient, industrious, persistent and conscientious.
>
> (Ashton, Kneen and Davies, 1975, p. 89)

'Individualistic' teachers emphasize

> children making reasoned judgements and choices and forming a considered opinion. . . . Related to this area but on a wider scale, these teachers want children to be able to plan independent work, organise their own time, to play a part in their own development by recognising their own strengths and limitations and setting their own goals and, of course, to be individuals, developing in their own way.
>
> (*Ibid.*)

Analytical distinctions of this kind have a limited value in suggesting the defining characteristics of broad categories of teachers; they do not explain why Ms A decides to regroup the classroom furniture into learning areas or why Mr B rejects first-hand experience in favour of mathematics texts. They do highlight the essential individuality of ideological beliefs in which personal and professional values co-mingle. How do teachers become child-centred, or reject child-centredness, and what do they understand by it?

Ideologies by their nature are essentially personal and individual rationales for action. They are acquired through classroom and school experience and by a process of testing and reconstruction. Primary teachers will have encountered child-centredness as the official ideology of their initial teacher-education course. Its relatively protected environment with its short block-experience periods in school by its nature limits the degree to which the ideology's claims can be tested in the practical setting. Also, it is realistic to suggest that student teachers may be reluctant to challenge or question what amounts to their course's central articles of faith, avowed by tutors responsible for assessing them, because of their weak position in the training institution's power structure. The problem of having to satisfy both the college's and the school's requirements while on teaching practice probably provides the student's first stage to developing a workable personal and professional ideology. New teachers entering their probationary years will display a wide range of responses to child-centredness but only now will they be able to test these against experience. The first concern of a probationary teacher is coming to terms with the realization that he or she is responsible for the education of thirty or so children for a whole year, considerably more challenging than having part-responsibility for a class under the – it is hoped – benevolent eye of an experienced teacher for six weeks. Establishing validity in the eyes of colleagues and superiors, inside and outside the school through exercising classroom organization skills and maintaining order will be the main priority. The rationales for action that develop, well beyond the probationary year, will be embedded in everyday practice rather than being a conscious justification. They tend to become explicit and put into words only when teachers are asked to reflect on their beliefs, or are challenged by a new set of conditions or a researcher. 'Mrs Carpenter' in Sharp and Green (1975) is a good example of a child-centred teacher trying to articulate her beliefs about the values and practices of primary teaching and to reconcile them with her low expectations of the children. She is fluent only when she describes instances of learning and teaching that illustrate her general position, which emphasizes the essentially practical and applied nature of personal ideologies.

These points suggest that there is no automatic connection between trying to be child-centred and promoting equality. If 'Mrs Carpenter', or the teachers in Lee's (1984) study are typical, the traditional expressions of the ideology become more entrenched the more they are seen to be unworkable in a 'blaming the victim' manoeuvre. Clearly, a teacher who claims to be child-centred and also claims that such an approach cannot work with 'this type of child' will be at odds when faced with equality imperatives. More positively, the majority of primary teachers who appear to reject child-centredness as an operable set of values possibly do so because of its inadequacy in the face of school and education-system practicalities. But its central concerns – its respect for the learner and emphasis on the development of human autonomy – should make it the most appropriate facilitating structure for developing equality.

Child-Centredness and Social Justice: an Attempted Reconciliation

It is argued here that traditional child-centredness of the kind King (1978) identified is inadequate because the social dimension is neglected in it: full account needs to be taken of the obvious and mundane point that we all are social creatures from birth. Better links, therefore, can be made between beliefs and practices when the social is as strong as the individualistic dimension; at the least, this will be a more convincing rationale for primary teaching at the initial preparation stage and therefore a firmer basis for developing personal ideological positions. In turn, a socially-oriented child-centredness should provide a basis for promoting equality, as suggested earlier. Alexander (1984, p. 31) draws attention to what he regards as the misleading dichotomy of 'child v. society': 'Clearly, the polarisation is untenable: the child is a member of society; so is the teacher. Society and the individual define each other'. He suggests that the dichotomy reflects an under-estimation of the cultural importance of teachers' classroom actions but his illustrations from child-centred theorists suggest rejection rather than this. The 'pure' version of the ideology also tends to be preserved by the insularity of many primary teachers, which helps to shield them from political and social realities affecting children, as Lee (1984) and Sharp and Green (1975) indicate.

These points challenge the protected environment of traditional child-centredness, in which such tenents as childhood innocence and natural goodness can be nourished, so long as the right type of child inhabits it. A tangible and everyday projection of this latter day Rousseauism is the rurality that permeates much primary practice, in inner-city schools as much as elsewhere: the covert belief that cities are alienating, environmentally repellent and corrupt, and that images of rurality brought into the classroom such as nature tables, growing daffodils and candytuft, harvest festivals, producing frogs and going on school journeys into the countryside, will somehow counteract the city's anti-educational influence. It is an evocation of Rousseau's education in Arcadia. It is not surprising, therefore, that primary-teacher training, and especially that for the early years, used to emphasize the expressive and creative arts as appropriate educational experiences to transfer into classrooms rather than technology, science and mathematics. In suburban schools, the rural myth can be sustained up to a point, since suburbs are compromise expressions of rurality. Where its assumptions are challenged most by physical and social conditions – in inner-city schools – some teachers adopt fallback positions in which the home environment is blamed for shortcomings in children's learning and social behaviour, as mentioned earlier. This deficit view was present even in some of the post-Plowden Educational Priority Area action research projects, in which the urban setting was supposed to be the mainspring for children's learning. In the Deptford project, an environmental-studies scheme using a field centre near Swanley was developed, for a range of reasons, conscious and unconscious, as Barnes (1975, p. 175) reveals:

> Everybody, it was assumed, 'knew' what the Environmental Studies scheme was about. As it transpired, I think, the scheme was about three things with an inevitable fourth only in the mid-distance. It was about children enjoying school. It was about providing experiences for children in urban EPA schools which a 'good parent' ought to provide. It was about offering children intrinsically worthwhile experiences. And in the distance was a further concern: for the school performance of the youngsters.

Another factor that promotes rather than expresses this kind of child-centredness lies in the enclosed nature of school buildings as enclaves of order, rationality and purposefulness in a chaotic and threatening world; Grace (1978) described Victorian elementary schools as citadel schools, physically excluded from their neighbourhoods by high brick walls, with entrances that were both hard to find and strictly categorized into 'boys', 'girls' and 'infants' and barred to parents. Of course, the buildings themselves have changed; although accessibility to schools by parents and others has increased enormously, especially in the past fifteen years, the basic purposes of schools remain the same, and they emphasize the special responsibility of the teacher: parents, at least ritually, hand over their children to be trained and educated by another adult, with varying degrees of parent–teacher collaboration agreed. Therefore, an ideology that emphasizes growth and experiential learning, justified by a belief in the naturalness of individual development, in turn supported by a belief in children's natural goodness, fits well with the exclusivity of schools and teachers. It provides a rationale for autonomy and privacy. Much the same, of course, can be claimed for alternative ideologies that stress character training, or the induction of children into socially-valued forms of knowledge.

Schooling is not an all-inclusive experience: children are members of society, at least when they are out of school. If the concern really is for 'the whole child', the educative function is not complete unless it includes the means by which children are increasingly made aware of the society in which they are growing up. Carrington and Short (1987) suggest that there is considerable resistance from primary teachers to presenting contentious social issues such as racism to children because of the imperatives of traditional child-centredness. In particular, Piaget's stage sequence – the basis of teachers' beliefs about sequential development – is often rigidly adhered to, which leads teachers to believe that anti-racist approaches, for example, are too abstract and difficult for primary children to understand. A teacher blockage linked to this is the feeling that children's natural innocence should be shielded from such threatening material. It follows that many primary teachers judge these social/political issues, which are crucial to the development of equality policies, in negative terms, as an intrusion on 'true' education – thus the child v. society dichotomy.

This social dimension to child-centredness, then, is crucially important to equality development. It means combining major developmental social/political factors concerning class and race membership and gender identity with traditional child-centredness's respect for individual development and autonomy. Arguably, the traditional expression of the ideology only becomes workable in schools and classrooms when teachers consciously or unconsciously restrict their vision. This reconsideration should not only give teachers an expanded referential framework for considering the 'whole child', but also make them more aware of social/political movements and influences (often in conflict) that seek to define such central issues as teachers' roles and professional status in the State system and what counts as school knowledge and achievement in terms of these.

If the notion of equality as an equal opportunity to achieve is taken to be a legitimate goal for schools to pursue, the argument so far suggests that much remains to be done, and that school achievement in Britain continues to be defined narrowly and distributed unevenly. There seem to be two approaches to tackling this problem: by trying to raise the level of achievement in its conventional form of tests and examinations; or by reconsidering what should count as achievement, following the ILEA Hargreaves and Thomas committees. The first approach is very much what the national curriculum and testing clauses in the Education Act 1988 are about, while the second seeks to redefine achievement so that practical, know-how type and personal/social skills are included. It will be argued here that the second approach is more in accord with equality goals and is not in itself in conflict with the first.

Child-Centredness and School Achievement

Equality of educational opportunity necessarily focuses on school achievement since equal access to education is a sham unless it is accompanied by equal opportunities to achieve. Thus the late nineteenth-century 'ladder of opportunity' scholarship device by which elementary school children could gain access to an academic secondary education aimed at identifying those few judged able enough to benefit from this. But the notion that equality of opportunity through education is based on the principle that children should not only have equal access to bodies of knowledge but also an equal right to achieve in school is essentially meritocratic rather than egalitarian, when achievement is defined narrowly in conventional academic terms as Jeffcoate (1984, p. 73) has pointed out. He argues in the context of the evidence for Afro-Caribbean children's under-achievement that

> The perversion of the equal opportunity philosophy, in the apparent interests of academics and employers, goes some way to explaining why those areas of school and public life in which West Indians have been conspicuously successful – sport, music, drama and dance – have been either disregarded by research or subjected to exclusively negative interpretations.

School achievement has been defined in academic conceptual terms from the beginnings of the public examination system in the 1850s. The motives for this are related both to utilitarian and egalitarian goals: that State education should be efficient, which emphasizes measurable learning and the transmission of socially-useful knowledge and skills, and that it should provide the means for upward mobility – though here, a government's aim of establishing a stable society built on successful personal ambition arguably lies behind the more altruistic goal. In any case, the two are closely linked because, since the State system is financed from public funds, an economic-investment view predominates in which the first goal is taken to be the more important. This tradition (promoting efficiency, cost effectiveness and raising measurable achievement standards) is expressed by the implementation of the national curriculum and bench-mark testing. It follows that equality in education has normally been couched in Crosland's (1962) 'weak' terms as the analysis in Chapter 3 argues, in which equality of opportunity means access by tests to high-status education. Since equality of opportunity is defined in these terms, of universal access but individual IQ-oriented performance in a class-based society, it is meritocratic and not egalitarian. An extension of this is the apparent contradiction that in this society it is possible to have access and to achieve highly but not to have equality of opportunity, because of the effects of institutionalized and personal prejudice, stereotyping and discrimination in the form of classism, racism and sexism.

The problem therefore is not only how achievement is defined but also the dominant institutional and personal values that largely determine who will be sponsored among those who do achieve. Schools as State institutions can do just so much in their pupils' interests. Even if the meritocratic charge can be countered, if equal access is the first step towards equality of opportunity, equal rights to achieve is only the second rather than the final step; but it might be the only feasible final step for schools. This reality is behind the equality policies of urban education authorities such as Brent, Haringey and ILEA, which have been taken to be radical and social engineering. Their anti-racism and anti-sexism are geared to raising educational performance in their schools, set in the context of these ills of society. In a similar, class-based context, equality to achieve was also the driving principle within Midwinter's (1972) work in the Liverpool 8 Educational Priority Area following the Plowden recommendations. Through a community-based curriculum, 'constructive discontent' would be generated in children, who would become the entrepreneurs and agents for social regeneration for their deprived areas. Their ability to negotiate on equal terms with powerful resource agencies outside would be based on their high level of conventional school achievement obtained through a conventional curriculum located in a community context. The fault in the process, as Midwinter conceded, was that there would also be those who would use their school success as an escape route since, implicit in his scheme, was the conviction that there would be no structural changes in society, only improvements to the status quo. In the same way, an 'outcome' as well as an 'intake' argument, linking individual achievement with post-education opportunity, can be used where equality policies take a conventional equal-opportunities form and are premised on raising the level of conventional achievement such as success in public examinations and entry to higher education. Their 'intake' meritocracy is reinforced, since it will be a matter of personal values and choice as to whether individual high achievers use their success to further social justice, or for personal ambition, or whether they have the opportunity to use it at all.

What if an expanded notion of achievement is incorporated into equal opportunities? School achievement takes its form because conventional educational wisdom has traditionally defined it as a product of inherited, genetically-determined intelligence. Therefore, because of the distribution of measurable intelligence across a population, in the recent past only a small proportion of children have been considered able enough to benefit from an academic secondary-level education. The continued existence of selective secondary schooling in several local authorities with entry controlled by the results of verbal-reasoning tests and secondary-transfer procedures based on ability banding confirms that this belief is still embedded in the State education system. It has been reinforced in the race context by the support it received through Jensen's (1969) and Eysenck's (1971) research. Thus, for example, the under-achievement of black children – whoever these are – compared with whites and most Asian groups is seen as inevitable by some teachers because of these children's supposed inherently lower intelligence; the research findings of Rex and Tomlinson (1979) and Little and Willey (1981) bear this out. This closed-circle thinking, which also applies to girls' abilities compared with boys, as Byrne (1978) and Spender (1980) confirm, operates in two ways that are analysed further in Chapter 2: through labelling certain groups of children and setting up stereotypes of expected behaviour, and by adopting a narrow definition of achievement that rests on traditional academic success only.

A process-based educational philosophy such as child-centredness is fundamentally at odds with a measurable-product view of achievement, if only because it identifies and assesses such a small part of a child's educational experience. If the definition was broadened to include applied, affective and collaborative learning as well as cognitive it would be possible to acknowledge the value of learning processes as well as outcomes. Such a broadening would also go a long way towards countering the meritocracy charge against equality of opportunity. Of course, while a broader notion of what counts as achievement would mean that many more children would experience success in school, there is no entailment that these kinds of success would be valued on a par with conventional achievement outside schools. In fact, there is the danger that it could be seen as a soft option for those who cannot compete, a spurious form of lower-level achievement.

The ILEA Thomas Report, *Improving Primary Schools* (1985), was the second of three major reports based on the authority's investigations into under-achievement conducted in the late 1970s. Its terms of reference are concerned with raising the achievement especially of working-class children and how this might be done through particular school strategies. The major concern here is with the committee's reconceptualizing of the nature of school achievement that the pioneering Hargreaves Report, *Improving Secondary Schools* (1982), recommended. Arguably, this is the focal point for both reports since all the recommendations concerning the curriculum, organization and teachers' roles depend on it for their realization. They comprise four aspects of achievement, which include a range of process and affective factors as well as more readily-measurable learning.

Achievement aspect I is strongly represented in the current 16-plus public examinations. It involves most of all the capacity to express oneself in a written form. It requires the capacity to retain propositional knowledge, to select from such knowledge appropriately in response to a specified request, and to do so quickly without reference to possible sources of information. The capacity to memorise and organise material is particularly important. Public examinations emphasise knowledge rather than skill; memorisation more than problem-solving or investigational capacities; writing rather than speaking or other forms of communication; speed rather than reflection; individual rather than group achievement.

Achievement aspect II is concerned with the capacity to apply knowledge rather than knowledge itself, with the practical rather than the theoretical, with the oral rather than the written. Problem-solving and investigational skills are more important than the retention of knowledge. This aspect has assumed greater importance in primary schools during recent decades. It tends to be more difficult, as well as more time-consuming to assess than aspect I.

Aspect III is concerned with personal and social skills; the capacity to communicate with others in face-to-face relationships; the ability to cooperate with others in the interests of the group as well as of the individual; initiative, self-reliance and the ability to work alone without close supervision; and the skills of leadership. Some parts of this aspect have been taken further in primary schools in recent years than formerly, but other parts, notably group cooperation, are still often an intention rather than a reality.

Achievement aspect IV involves motivation and commitment; the willingness to accept failure without destructive consequences; the readiness to persevere; the self-confidence to learn in spite of the difficulty of the task. Such motivation is often regarded as a prerequisite to achievement, rather than as an achievement in itself. Like the Hargreaves Committee, we accept that motivation is a prerequisite to the other three aspects of achievement. We, also, believe that it can be regarded as an achievement in its own right. It has to be generated by schools, and in the case of some pupils, mainly by schools. Aspect IV is of particular importance for some working class pupils, though not to them only.

(Thomas, 1985, p. 2)

Since they express many contextual and process-related learning factors that teachers recognize and value, they are not a radical reconstruction. But they do pose a number of problems and questions of interpretation and use. First, while the committee argues that the distinctions between them are analytical only, since they are meant to focus on different aspects of a child's performance, they could be interpreted as being separate, with teachers planning their programmes so as to satisfy 'Thomas aspect III', for instance; the author has circumstantial evidence to suggest that some teachers do see them in discrete terms. Of course, this might be a first step towards understanding and implementing the redefinition and emphasizing what might have been neglected. Second, the way they are ordered could result in their being perceived as a hierarchy of achievement by teachers and parents. Perhaps it is no accident that the traditional interpretation is placed first and the most tenuous fourth with exhortations that the committee regards it as being the most important. Certainly, I and II are conventional forms of achievement capable of being assessed, but are aspects III and IV anything more than a description of the conditions needed for achieving in the first two modes? Third, these problems of relationship and status are heightened by the cognitive orientation of aspects I and II and the affective nature of III and IV; what is more problematic in this is the suggestion that the strongly-attitudinal aspect IV is especially relevant to working-class children, which might confirm a deficit-type justification for these children's achievement potential for those who seek this.

But they represent, at least potentially, a 'whole-child' approach to achievement, applicable to all primary children. They would not be unfamiliar to virtually all nursery and infant teachers, in a tacit, less-elaborated form. The problem remains of how to get the majority of teachers to accept them, in terms of the implicit child-centred philosophy in which they are located and, more practically, in the face of bench-mark testing on a national scale. They would require a more elaborate form of record-keeping than a cumulative list of reading-age and mathematics attainment scores with comments on a child's interests and activities throughout a year. A profile approach, which is now fairly common in local authorities and which includes examples of a child's work across the curriculum and at different times in the year, including teachers' and others' observations, would be suitable. It also serves to emphasize the breadth of information needed if a child's achievement is to be appraised realistically. None of this will, of course, convince teachers who have an ingrained performance belief about achievement, but for most teachers, the increased and more precise observations they will need to make about each child's activities, relationships, interests and measurable performance in order to compile a profile should at least draw their attention to the complex and holistic nature of individual achievement. In doing this, they are likely to become more aware of particular children's strengths, weaknesses, personal dispositions and attitudes that make up the contexts and conditions according to which each child progresses or has difficulties in school. They are also likely to become more aware of their own attitudes and expectations regarding particular children and how these influence individual progress.

A reconceptualization of child-centredness reinforced by a broader view as to what counts as achievement can provide the basic terms of reference within which equality as a practical principle becomes part of each child's learning experience. But the reality is that by the time children enter school, their social attitudes are already well developed. This suggests a number of constraints for schools trying to raise achievement levels and to develop life chances, which are considered in the next chapter.

2
SOCIAL JUSTICE
AND EARLY SOCIALIZATION

Children's attitudes concerning race and gender are largely formed before they enter school and contribute to the development of stereotypes concerning behaviour and school performance. The links between attitudes and achievement are strong, but the research coverage is uneven, especially in the case of the achievement of children in ethnic minority groups. Teachers' attitudes transmitted as learning expectations are also important in promoting or inhibiting achievement. Together, these factors portray some of the constraints and the possibilities that influence the development of race and sex equality in primary schools.

The Development of Attitudes

It is a truism that education is concerned with rationality and the development of rational and responsible human beings. It is also true that because children's pre-school socialization is relatively uncontrolled and varied, they have to be 'schooled' both in the interests of subsequent individual development and in order that they can develop in clearly-defined rule-governed conditions. Faced with this diversity of entry characteristics, teachers of young children often equate their children's basic social competence with their ability to understand and to accept the goals of schooling. Being toilet trained and being able to do up buttons and shoe-laces go with good attitudes such as being receptive to learning tasks. Social attitudes that involve less-visible aspects of the culture are another dimension, which –

Equality Issues in Primary Schools

though they may be less obvious to teachers – have a profound effect on children's abilities to learn. As Milner (1983, p. 53) points out, 'For in the socialisation process, children learn not only "what to do" but also "how things are" as "we" see them. Learning the business of living in a culture is not only a question of learning skills but also learning *meanings*'. Children have to be active participants in this early learning. They are impelled to interpret what they experience in order to cope with the mass of confusing information bombarding them from their parents, the street, other children and adults and the media well before they go to school. Inevitably, parents are the main instruments of the socialization process, as instructors and role models; their attitudes to different races and their beliefs and portrayals of gender roles will be authoritative. Early social attitudes and the prejudices and stereotypes associated with them, and which they assimilate, are therefore the mechanisms young children use against the unpredictability of the world, and the anxiety and helplessness this causes. They are born out of powerlessness and lack of experience: security and continuity come from aligning oneself with those who have power. Therefore, it is not surprising that parents will be the most influential figures in a young child's life and that their values and beliefs will become the child's own. These will also be potent and resistant to challenge because they represent security. Racial and gender stereotypes concerning behaviour and appearance define and reinforce individual identity at a point when this is most vulnerable, by identifying what are taken to be appropriate beliefs and behaviour. Again, the distribution of power in a society, as experienced by children, is the major influence as to which stereotypes are assimilated and how they are operated. Milner's analysis (*ibid*. p. 53) in a racial-attitudes context has a universal application:

> we have to consider the various sources of information and emotion in a relatively restricted social world. This world is bounded by the home, the street, the school and the mass media, yet within these limits the child will learn most of what he or she needs to know about the world. . . . All the ways of doing things practised in the immediate group or the wider culture are conveyed to children, intentionally and by accident, with or without their realisation. And the process begins at birth; the notion that children begin to absorb the culture with their mother's milk is certainly no exaggeration.

He maintains that there are three overlapping processes at work: direct tuition, indirect tuition and role learning. Parents are instrumental in the direct tuition process through the ways in which they instruct their children in correct attitudes. As for indirect tuition, parents are still powerful influences through the models of attitude and behaviour they provide for their children to assimilate and reproduce, with identification and modelling being the two modes of expression. Role learning is the linking mechanism by which children are inducted as active members of different social groups. It overlaps with direct and indirect tuition in the manner in which behaviour, which at first is individual and personal, becomes both the expression of social identity and the means by which it is developed.

These early acquired attitudes are reinforced by the culture in a number of ways. Milner stresses the inevitability of the process, in the way it reproduces dominant attitudes in the young and their reinforcement by such cultural influences as children's books and comics and school learning resources, including reading schemes.

Children's Racial Attitudes

The inevitability of attitudes development also applies to the perpetuation of racial attitudes through the transmission of deep-seated assumptions – virtually folk memories – about blacks and foreigners, which seem to have their origins in the heyday of the British Empire, colonialism and slavery. Rex (1973), quoted in Tierney (1982), firmly locates racism in the colonial period as being a means by which the imperial powers justified their colonial exploitation by using biologically-based race supremacy arguments drawing upon Darwinism. Bash, Coulby and Jones (1985, pp. 94–5) expand this argument by suggesting three reasons as to why racism persists well beyond the break-up of the empire:

> First, the myth that the British gave independence willingly to the former constituent parts of the Empire: that is, just as the British acquired it for high-minded reasons, so they relinquished it for equally unselfish motives. . . . Secondly, having lost political and, increasingly, economic domination over an Empire, the British still maintain a belief in a moral ascendency over the Commonwealth as it is now called, particularly the so-called 'new' Commonwealth (i.e. black) countries. . . . Thirdly, and perhaps most important of all, the view . . . that black people were childlike, ignorant and capable of only menial jobs, the 'Africa never invented the wheel' syndrome.

An effective recent example of all three at work, though not quite as described above, can be seen in the government and media treatment of Colonel Rambuka's *coup* in Fiji, in which the simple Fijians are seen to usurp the industrious, economically dominant and more-cultured Indian population, and in which the Queen as Head of the Commonwealth is set aside with the establishment of a republic.

Cashmore and Troyna (1983, cited in Cohen and Cohen, 1986, p. 93) also explore the assumed natural-superiority arguments used when one group of people successfully exert power over another and how these are detached from scientific analyses:

> Race and inequality are, as we shall see, intimately connected – perfect partners. The scientific bases on which the ideas of race rest may be disinterested and detached from the issues of inequality, but there again, race is not simply the preserve of academics. It is when it is in the hands, or, more accurately, heads of 'men-in-the-street' that it takes on its more powerful form.

They go on to link racism with the inherent inequalities of capitalism. It is used as a weapon of exploitation by the ruling group to create and to maintain antagonisms between groups of workers:

> The capitalists' heaviest weapon is open racial conflict when groups organize their allegiances along perceived racial lines and clash with those of other races. But at a covert level, a simmering or latent conflict is also useful in preventing the workers from perceiving their real allegiances – with each other – and their real opposition – the capitalist class.
>
> (*Ibid.* p. 102)

The Marxist argument, about race as an instrument of oppression, is strong on structure but weak on psychology; it says little about how membership of a particular human group leads to consciousness of race and to that of racial superiority. Are the sources of racism to be found simply in an inherent distrust of the unfamiliar, which, therefore, becomes threatening? If so, the rest is justification: fear of the unfamiliar must be given a concrete form for it to be fully identified and neutralized, so race prejudice in the form of antipathy to a different skin colour and facial features is extended to body odour – actual or imagined – and then to cultural-identity factors such as diet, clothes, family composition and religion. This is transmuted to racism and to its active form, racialism, when one race group in a society has the power to discriminate against and to oppress another group. The temperature, as it were, of racism in a society can be taken by listening to children and young people who often express racism in a particularly unadulterated way as some of pupils quoted by Gaine (1987) graphically demonstrate.

Prejudice and its expressions and justifications is therefore at the root of racism and to the attitudes to race children acquire. Milner's historical account (1983, p. 7) of how prejudice has operated in different societies focused on the rejection of black people by white, in which the perjorative associations of 'black' were (and still are) reinforcers and expressions of prejudice:

> The association of blackness with evil is a common theme both historically and cross-culturally. 'Black' had a highly perjorative connotation in England in and before the sixteenth century. Its meanings included 'deeply stained with dirt,

soiled, dirty, foul . . . having dark or deadly purposes, malignant; deadly, disastrous, sinister' and so on. White has a correspondingly pure connotation.

He then considers how prejudice acquired scientific respectability through the work of early social psychologists who ascribed certain supposed racial characteristics to different groups. He cites Edward Ross' *Social Psychology*, published in 1907, that describes 'negro volubility, Singalese treachery, Magyar passion for music', which are claimed to arise from race endowment. White Caucasians provided the essential basis for comparison with other races, not the least because most of the early social psychologists were white Caucasians. Allport in the USA caused a major shift in this line of thinking through his claim that social and not biological causes were behind the oppression suffered by Negroes. The line of development proceeds from a concern with individual responses to the phenomenon of difference, expressed through prejudiced behaviour, to an increasing interest in its group and social nature. This move became especially important with the growth of totalitarian regimes in Europe in the 1920s and 1930s and the migration movements following the Second World War.

Perhaps the most chilling aspect of Milner's study is the evidence he uses to demonstrate the embeddedness of white children's racial attitudes from the age of 3 or 4 years – well before they are old enough to go to school. Much of the research evidence he cites derives from doll-play experiments. While the attitudes themselves are made vividly clear by his reportage, it is less clear how children move from acquiring attitudes to using these to ascertain their own status and that of others.

> What is less easy to tease out is the origin of hostile feelings, the actual emotional, evaluative thrust behind rejecting attitudes. To say that they are modelled from the parents is not quite adequate; it implies a passive process, which can explain how children learn what they should feel about things, but not actually how they come to feel them themselves.
>
> (*Ibid*. p. 111)

He suggests that a major mechanism here is the way children are inducted by their parents at a very early age into the positive/negative polarities of such opposites as good/bad, white/black, yes/no, smiling/frowning, through such prohibitions as not touching fires, cookers, electric sockets and valued possessions. The 'no' concept and the disapproval it communicates at a pre-verbal level, before the child has acquired any language, is a powerful shaping influence. The young child starts to apply the 'no' concept to the more indirect and subtle expressions of parental disapproval such as tone, gesture, expressions and inflexions, and to connect them to their causes. Through this alignment process, children acquire their parents' prejudices in a prejudiced society; it is a crucial source of approval and security. This development continues at a slower rate in older children with some levelling off in early adolescence. For example, differentiation may occur in which a white child might like a black child but be prejudiced against black people as a group. A further, overarching factor is the tendency for authoritarian personalities and members of families having an authoritarian climate to be drawn to racism.

So far as black children are concerned, earlier research evidence suggests that they have a highly-positive orientation towards whites and a correspondingly low regard for blacks. This is reinforced by social status as Cashmore and Troyna (1983) argue: that racial inequalities are used by minority groups to define and confirm their own low status. Where skin colour is underscored by political and economic inferiority, the subordination of black to white in children's minds will be more pronounced. As with white children, doll-play research has been an important instrument. Some of the research discussed by Milner suggests that race awareness and its implications develops earlier in black compared with white children; studies in the 1950s and 1960s revealed various forms of rejection of black identity such as blacks being losers or the 'baddies' in stories to be completed. All of this might suggest a certain inevitability of development of negative black self-concepts, with possible school achievement consequences. But this is untrue: Milner cites research done in the early 1970s in the USA and the late 1970s in Britain in which the black subjects showed a decline in white preference and misidentification. However, as a consequence of this earlier research, a causal relationship between negative self-images, actual or assumed, and under-achievement has been established in the minds of many teachers as part of their common-sense understanding, especially in inner-city multiracial schools, as Lee (1984) suggests. It is akin to earlier teacher assumptions about the effects of home background on children's learning, based on research in the 1950s and 1960s and presented in initial teacher-education courses, in which a similarly deterministic view was taken about the low potential of working-class children. Plowden's preoccupation with the 'cultural deprivation' of most working-class children as a result of their being brought up in homes not geared to schooling gave this viewpoint a lasting authority for many primary teachers; it became as much a part of their professional ideology as Piaget's stages. Its determinism and that of its more recent race counterpart derives from the belief that the home influence will always be stronger than the school's, which renders schools and teachers powerless to intervene. Because these situations are taken for granted, almost as part of the natural order, such teachers do not see them to be essentially prejudiced standpoints, respectively operating against working-class and black children, as projections of classism and racism in society.

Stone's (1981) criticism of so-called multiracial education, or MRE, focuses on its acceptance of the link between low self-concept and under-achievement; MRE is a deficit compensatory perspective because it aims at raising supposedly-low self-concepts through an alternative, low-status, expressive arts-based education rather than trying to raise achievement by challenging black children via the mainstream academic curriculum. Clearly there are important implications here for teachers in relation to the perform-ance and later life chances of ethnic-minority children that will be discussed later in this chapter.

Children's Gender Attitudes

As Meighan (1986) points out, children receive a sex-differentiation label at birth through their first names. As with race, the pattern of stereotypes about masculinity and femininity is founded on the assumption of biological differences that are manifested in appropriate social behaviour. Thus there is the same closed-circle pattern of reasoning in which gender-related behaviour is taken to be a normal and natural projection of male and female biology. The issues of inequality and discrimination are no less clear than they are for race, but the processes that sustain gender inequalities are that much more embedded in British society. Is it because sex membership is seen to be more basic to someone's identity than race membership? For example, Watts (1988) claims that sexual harassment and abuse as an expression of male sexuality continues to be offered as a compliment or a joke and not perceived as a deterrent to women's equality. As she describes, the male bullying and manipulation invoked in calling girls 'frigid' or 'slags' is repeated even in situations where women have some power: When (as rarely happens) women MPs sat together to oppose John Corrie's amend-ment to the abortion Bill, their male colleagues jeered at them in the language of prostitution – "Who's the madame?" "How much for two?" – then accused them of having no sense of humour' (*Ibid.* p. 34). Clearly, they share only formal equality with their male counterparts, a point that Deem (1978, p. 22) makes in considering the structural force of biological and social attempts to legitimize women's ascribed roles in society: 'Because women in capitalist societies have a different and subordinate position in the division of labour compared with men, some of the knowledge, skills, values and ideas presented in schools are of no use to women, except as confirma-tion of their position in the sexual division of labour'.

These preconceptions are embedded in such influential research as the Newsoms' study of infant care as Deem claims, in the way they explained variations in sex-stereotyped behaviour between 4-year-old and 7-year-old

children. The Newsoms' explanation that older children have more autonomy than younger children implicitly accepts such behaviour as being
natural by ignoring the greater pressure on the younger children to conform:
'This reflects an implicit assumption by the Newsoms that sex differences in
behaviour are innate so that when children are allowed to choose their own
activities they choose those which are in accordance with their membership
of a particular sex' (*ibid.* p. 31).

In fact, research findings reveal few differences between males and
females apart from obvious physiological differences concerned with repro-
duction. Jayne's (1984, p. 2) survey of research suggests

> Firstly that there are fewer than we suppose for when studies are conducted of
> how girls and boys or women and men actually think and act, they are remarkably
> similar ('remarkable' only . . . because it is the differences we tend to notice, not
> similarities). Furthermore differences we suppose exist often are not substanti-
> ated by research evidence. Thus Eleanor Macoby and Carol Jacklin's book *The
> Psychology of Sex Differences*, 1975 reviewing thousands of studies failed to find
> evidence to support the widely held view that there were differences in social
> orientation, suggestability, self-esteem, cognitive or analytic ability. Nor were
> there consistent differences between the sexes on measures of anxiety, level of
> activity, competitiveness, dominance, compliance or nurturance.

She cites a later study by Macoby and Jacklin (1980) that suggests that actual
differences revealed have to be evaluated in terms of distribution overlaps
between male and female samples, the fact that most studies are of white
middle-class American children, that research which detects differences
tends to be published before research that does not, and that detected
differences are often assumed to be natural – that is, unlearnt. Macoby and
Jacklin's research does suggest there are boy–girl differences in verbal
ability with girls showing superiority from 11 years in vocabulary, reading
comprehension, verbal fluency, verbal analogies and opposites and verbal-
reasoning problems. In mathematics, boys from 11 to 18 years make more
rapid progress although boys and girls learn to count and to understand
number conservation at about the same age. In visual/spatial ability, boys
achieve higher scores from 11–13 years of age.

Deem's review of research reveals that boys and girls do acquire different
skills and aptitudes that are reinforced and reflected in their school achievements. Simultaneously, they learn the appropriate gender-related manner
in which to express emotion, manage conflicts and develop relationships.
Oakley's work (1982, cited in Jayne, 1984) suggests that gender identity is
fixed in the first two years, and that children know whether they are girls or
boys before they can relate this to genital sex differences; also that the ways
parents distinguish between daughters and sons is insufficient as an explanation of the separate feminine and masculine self-concepts that develop.

Early in life, these mutually-reinforcing aspects of development, which in turn are reinforced by the family, peers and the media, become taken for granted by boys and girls as normal behaviour. The gender identity, in Danziger's (1971) terms, that children acquire, is the basis on which they evaluate themselves and other people. It follows that this identity, since it embodies the distribution of power and esteem in a male-oriented society, early on establishes the dominance of boys over girls in such life-chances determining areas as school achievement and career aspirations. Schools and teachers reflect this inequality in such areas as learning resources (for example, Lobban's (1978) research into the sexist nature of reading schemes); in the passivity expected of girls in question-and-discussion activities (for example, Spender (1980)), and in achievement expectations in high-status subjects such as mathematics, for example, Sharma and Meighan (1980).

Clarricoates' study (1980) of teachers' stereotypes in four primary schools confirms this power and expectations framework that operates through both the overt and the hidden curriculum in a classroom. Teachers used the following to describe the different characters and personalities of boys and girls as pupils (*ibid*. p. 39):

GIRLS	BOYS
Obedient,	Livelier
Tidy	Adventurous
Neat	Aggressive
Conscientious	Boistrous
Orderly	Self-confident
Fussy	Independent
Catty	Energetic
Bitchy	Couldn't-care-less
Gossiping	Loyal

Four out of the nine girls' characteristics are negative, in contrast to the boys' one, mildly, negative.

It will be clear that factors such as identity acquisition, self-concept and socialization patterns, on the one hand, and labelling, prejudice, discrimination and differential expectations on the other, not only play a part in depressing the school achievement of ethnic-minority children and girls, but also can be used to explain and to justify this lower achievement. It was argued in the previous chapter that equality of educational opportunity is necessarily concerned with publically-esteemed achievement, because equal access to schooling is meaningless unless it is accompanied by equal opportunities to achieve. The links between high achievement in the education system and upward mobility hardly need arguing for any more. However, in a society in which there is racism, sexism and classism, achievement opportunities on offer will not necessarily lead to greater life chances; whether teachers see this as deterministic or a modifiable condition in an imperfect society rests on their own beliefs and values. Whatever these might be, teachers are agents of their children's best interests, and most would agree that these are best served by promoting children's abilities and achievement. They may also take the view that this is as far as they can go within the system, while at the same time fully acknowledging the achievement–opportunities link.

Life Chances and Achievement: Race and Gender

The Swann Committee reviewed research evidence on the under-achievement of Afro-Caribbean children and commissioned a survey of school-leavers in several multi-ethnic local authorities that suggested that they did less well in examinations than their white and Asian peers. It also enlisted two eminent academic psychologists to consider whether or not Afro-Caribbean under-achievement was caused by low intelligence. The background to this question was Jensen's (1969) paper that claimed that intelligence was 80 per cent inherited and only 20 per cent attributable to environmental factors. He went on to claim that USA blacks scored on average 15 points lower in intelligence tests than whites. Eysenck's work in Britain (1971), which also claimed that intelligence was largely innate, came to similar conclusions. Hebb's (1979) and Bynner's (1980) critiques respectively attacked Jensen's controlling for environmental influences such as social class, and his research methodology. But the Swann researchers (DES, 1985b) concluded that socio-economic factors are the main explanation of the difference in average IQ scores between Afro-Caribbean and white children. When this is taken into account, the differences are reduced by at least 50 per cent.

Cohen and Cohen's (1986) analysis of *Education for All* draws attention to how little is known about this area of school achievement. There is a need, they claim, for improved statistics on a national basis in order to identify its scale and to evaluate the ameliorative strategies being used in schools and local authorities. They make the point in support of socio-economic causes that while under-achievement might be affected by prejudice in schools, there is a much stronger connection between the effects of racism on socio-economic status through discrimination in employment and housing and under-achievement. Also, they cite Parekh's (1983) rebuttal of the claimed single-clause explanation of under-achievement. Parekh cited six suggested causes – in summary: genetically-caused lower intelligence; family structure not geared to schooling goals; economic and cultural disadvantage; the effects of racism; misguided and low expectations of schools; and the failure of education agencies to identify and meet distinctive needs. About the first, he says (Runnymeade Research Report, 1985, p. 5):

> First, the debate is vitiated by what I might call the fallacy of the single factor. The participants tend to look for one specific factor, be it class, racism, West Indian family, West Indian culture, the school or educational system, to explain the fact of underachievement. This is obviously an inherently impossible enterprise. Not even a relatively simple natural phenomenon like the falling of an apple or the dropping of a stone can be explained in terms of a single cause.

Parekh's analysis provides a comprehensive research framework for investigating the achievement of different pupil groups. It also draws attention to the highly-differentiated nature of ethnic-minority groups whether of West-Indian or Indian subcontinent origin. Some of the more-specific research information available compares girls' and boys' performance. For example, the Afro-Caribbean girls who Driver (1980) researched achieved as highly as their white female peers and higher than Afro-Caribbean boys. The ILEA-based *Fifteen Thousand Hours* research carried out by Rutter *et al.* (1979) also indicates the tendency for Afro-Caribbean pupils (especially girls), compared with white pupils, to stay on for a sixth year of secondary schooling. This transforms their examination performance: of the main research group of pupils in 1976, 1 per cent of Afro-Caribbeans gained five or more O-levels or grade-one CSEs compared with 7 per cent of white pupils, but when the extra year is taken into account, 19 per cent of Afro-Caribbeans compared with 11 per cent of whites gained this result, with 47 per cent of Afro-Caribbeans compared with 24 per cent of whites staying on.

The research suggests, therefore, that while some Afro-Caribbean pupils' earlier schooling is marked by underperformance, especially in language skills, girls especially – when they stay on – achieve results on a par with or above those of their Asian and white peers. If, as is likely, a higher proportion of Afro-Caribbean than white or Asian families are affected adversely by socio-economic conditions, their children's performance in school says much about the positive effects of schooling. It a'so indicates that, in line with Parekh, and contrary to Jensen and Eysenck, inherited intelligence is distributed evenly through the population regardless of race origins. As Jeffcoate (1984, p. 61) asks, 'How much Asian "overachievement" and West Indian "underachievement" is left once social class has been controlled for?'

While racism in Britain has its origins in the colonial period, sexism by its nature is rooted in the social structure. Division of role and labour by gender is one of the most basic social-organization mechanisms; sexism occurs when the pattern is perpetuated beyond its utility and where this inequality is both maintained and justified by the dominant sex. It is evident in the different life chances of boys and girls in British society. Deem's (1978) review of research evidence reveals that girls' levels of general intelligence is higher than that of boys before they begin school, but that the position slowly reverses as their school careers develop. Meighan (1986, p. 304) summarized the poorer educational life chances of girls compared with boys as follows:

1. Fewer girls than boys reach university.
2. Fewer girls than boys take GCE 'A' levels.
3. Fewer girls than boys take 'A' levels in physics, maths and chemistry.
4. Fewer girls that boys gain apprenticeships with linked further study.
5. Fewer females than males pursue the second-chance route of an Open University course, although the gap has closed.
6. Fewer boys than girls prepare for teacher education.

These figures are confirmed by ILEA's research underpinning its equal-opportunities policy. While it noted an increase in the proportion of girls taking O-levels in mathematics, physics and chemistry, this was not repeated at A-level (see Table 2.1). This division in subject choice also applies to the non-science subjects, except for biology, at CSE, O- and A-level (see Table 2.2). The national figures for these three examinations for 1979 show a similar distribution. The problem is not one of academic attainment but of representation, since girls' performance matches that of boys, even in subjects like physics where the girl-examinee proportion is small. The claimed causes are socio-cultural and institutional:

Girls, on the other hand, are clustered in the sectors where skills and functions are closely associated with the servicing role women also expect to perform within the family, such as education, nursing, catering and secretarial work. Nine years after

Table 2.1   A-level entries, maths, physics, chemistry, 1983

A-level	Girls (%)	Boys (%)
Maths	30	70
Physics	26	74
Chemistry	38	62

(*Source*: ILEA, 1985a, p. 5.)

Table 2.2   Examination entries, ILEA, 1983

	CSE		O-levels		A-levels	
	Girls (%)	Boys (%)	Girls (%)	Boys (%)	Girls (%)	Boys (%)
Biology	70	30	62	38	64	36
English	51	49	55	45	76	25
French	67	33	62	38	80	20
Home economics	91	9	90	10	100	Nil

(*Source*: ILEA, 1985a, p. 5.)

the Equal Pay and Sex Discrimination Acts came into force, women still earn on average less than three quarters of what men earn, and the gap is now widening again; the labour market is still highly sex-segregated; women represent a far greater proportion of the low-paid than men; and women still overwhelmingly dominate the part-time work force.

(ILEA, 1985a, p. 6)

And:

Women have less money, power, prestige, status and say than men. (Their earnings were 66% of men's last year; of people earning £500 a week or more, only six per cent were women.)

There are still infinitely fewer women than men who are successful financiers, politicians, philosophers, conductors, chefs, jockeys, pilots, editors, scientists or train-drivers; or who are eminent enough at anything to merit an entry in 'Who's Who'. Women compose almost half the country's workforce but only 10 per cent of its general managers, seven per cent of its senior civil servants, two per cent of its surgeons, three per cent of its judges, eight per cent of its chartered accountants.

Most women in Britain now work outside the home, but they also still do most of the work inside the home. In almost 90% of households the woman does the washing and ironing; in almost 75 per cent, she does the cleaning; in 70 per cent, she makes the supper. Women have fewer hours of leisure than men; their standard of living is lower than men's; at all ages, they run a greater risk of poverty than men. Half of all families living on or below the poverty line are headed by lone mothers, though such families compose only 12 per cent of all families with dependent children.

(Watts, 1988, p. 33–4)

What of girls in primary schools? The evidence suggests that the hidden curriculum operating in a classroom both draws upon and reinforces the sex roles developed in early socialization. Teachers expect girls to behave better than boys; Whyte's (1983) observations in a nursery school showed that if a boy broke something or struck someone, teachers were three times more likely to notice than if a girl did the same. The tendency was for a boy to be told off, loudly and publically, and for the girl to get a quiet rebuke. She suggests that while teachers and parents see their actions as making boys stand up for themselves and protecting girls, the boys actually form the view that teachers prefer girls to boys, which works as a self-fulfilling prophecy affecting approved and disapproved behaviour. She suggests that in fact teachers prefer boys for their liveliness and often have higher learning expectations of them; while girls are good at most things as a group, brilliance is expected of individual boys. It follows that girls' learning shortcomings are put down to stupidity while boys are accused of laziness. She cites one study where teachers blamed lack of motivation for boys' failures eight times more often than they did with girls. The consequence, she argues, is that while boys gain confidence and learn to be persistent, girls learn to be helpless.

Clarricoates (1983) comes to similar conclusions. The number of routines in school carried out by boys and girls separately (lining up for entering and leaving the classroom, playground, assembly, for school dinners) is criteria for appropriate behaviour, indicating to boys and girls that teachers identify them by gender. This is emphasized by class-control and organization mechanisms teachers use in expectation that disruption will come from the boys and not from the girls. These have the effect of reducing interaction and of setting up boy–girl competitiveness and antagonism. Also – since the boys are seen as the problem – many of the learning activities, such as projects, are oriented to them. Teachers' comments included: 'I do tend to try to make the topics as interesting as possible for the boys so that they won't lose their concentration' and 'Because girls settle down to their work better than the boys I naturally aim a topic at the boys' (*ibid.* p. 10). This has the effect of reinforcing the belief, both for children and teachers, that boys and girls have different natural skills and abilities in particular subjects. She agrees with Whyte about teachers' anticipations of behaviour, reinforced by the belief that girls are more reliable than boys when carrying out classroom tasks.

French and French's observational research of infant classrooms (French, 1986) revealed that there are marked behaviour differences between boys and girls, even with reception children. She cites the everyday practice of teachers gathering their children together on the carpet for news, stories, discussion, and so on. The boys invariably are more visible than the girls because of where and how they are seated: on the edge of the group, kneeling up or on chairs, compared with the girls, who usually sit cross-legged in the middle. They comment (p. 105) that

> The teacher, seated on a chair, above the level of the children, finds her natural line of gaze falling on the margins of the group, that is on the boys. She literally overlooks the girls in the body of the class. Pupils chosen to speak in the lesson are

then more often found to be those positioned at the boundaries rather than the centre – and thus to be boys.

While the boys in the thirty classes observed were proactive in demanding the teachers' attention, girls were perceived to be model pupils in the situation, not interrupting, raising their hands for attention – being unproblematic. They make the same point as Clarricoates, that teachers respond to their pupils' inputs, which essentially means that they respond to the boys.

Teachers have first to see these situations as being problematic as a condition for trying to reverse them through conscious strategies – also the necessary basis for operating an equality policy in a school. Hazel Taylor's (1987) example of a junior-class teacher demonstrating the superior physical strength of the girls in her class following a dispute raised by the boys is a case in point. Children can be rearranged in a group, as French points out. But it is difficult, as she suggests, for teachers to give less attention to restless or disruptive children, or not to respond to enthusiastic children if they are boys.

Teachers' Expectations: Race and Gender

Much has already been said about these from a pupil perspective in connection with achievement and life chances. Such expectations are undoubtedly powerful: Meighan (1986) takes the central proposition of teacher-expectation studies to be that pupils tend to perform as well or as badly as their teachers expect, and this is influenced by how nearly they fit the teacher's construction of the 'successful pupil'. Clarricoates' (1980) list of boys' characteristics as school pupils can be taken as a specification. Nash (1973) used a repertory-grid approach in identifying the constructs used by Scottish primary and secondary teachers; he asked them to describe how specific children in their classes differed from each other. From his comparisons of the behaviour and achievement of each pupil with their teacher's description, he concluded the pupils' attainment was strongly influenced by the way they were perceived. Rosenthal's (1973) survey of teacher-expectation research mentioned in Milner (1983) suggests there are four ways in which teachers can communicate their expectations: first, by creating a warm or cold climate – through tone of voice, smiling and extra verbal signals – they can bestow or withhold warmth, attention and support; second, through regulating feedback of acknowledgement and praise to approved and disapproved-of pupils; third, through the input of more and more difficult learning material; and, fourth, through regulating output – the number of questions asked, time to respond and guidance given.

From such studies it is fairly easy to deduce that the successful pupil is male, middle class, extrovert, white, relates well to adults in a non-subservient way, possesses developed standard English, has definite interests mostly in line with the school's goals and is intelligent – also according to how the school defines this.

Rubovits and Maehr's work (1973) tends to confirm these points from the race viewpoint. They studied experimental lessons in multiracial classrooms taken by student teachers; the children were of similar ability but half were represented by the researchers as 'gifted'. From their observations of teachers' behaviour, they found that white 'gifted' children were given the most attention and praise and the least criticism. They were also found to be the best liked by the teachers. The 'non-gifted' white children and black children were second and third in favour. The 'gifted' black children were therefore the least favoured. Although all the teachers were white, similar results were obtained in another study with black teachers. This, of course, is unequivocal racism – only white children are allowed to be high achievers. Cohen and Cohen (1986) describe an observational study of seventy teachers in four multiracial intake middle schools undertaken by Green (1982). Observations focused on how much time each teacher interacted with the class as a whole and with individual European, Afro-Caribbean and Asian children. Teachers were then rated on a racial tolerance–intolerance scale on the basis of observations plus an attitude inventory scale administered. Green concluded that highly-intolerant teachers (twelve out of the seventy) gave less time to accepting the feelings of Afro-Caribbean children, gave minimal praise, less attention to ideas they contributed, used direct teaching methods less with them, gave them more authoritative directions and less time for them to contribute to class discussions.

These research findings raise the crucial, and unpalatable, question of how far such racism is represented among teachers. In Britain, attempts to answer this question have been compromised in different ways. For example, the history of the Schools Council/NFER Education for a Multiracial Society Project demonstrates how political pressures can be brought to bear when controversial claims about teacher attitudes are made rather than neatly-packed curricular 'solutions' are delivered. The history of the project illustrates the virtual truism that if real change is to happen, teacher development has to proceed alongside curricular development. The project was initially concerned with producing multicultural curricular materials; the team concluded that because many teachers were unaware of or insensitive to race issues the materials would probably be misused. When the project report was published it was attacked by the media and teacher unions for claiming that teachers were racist; it was rejected in this form by the Schools Council and a moderate version was published later, from which many project-team members disassociated themselves.

The project at least drew attention to how little research there was on teachers' race attitudes, which was reasserted by the Rampton/Swann Committees. Their analysis, within cultural-pluralist parameters, also illustrates the elusiveness of the concept, although they condemn it unequivocally. The reports distinguish between intentional, unintentional and institutional racism. Intentional racism consists of motivated and organized beliefs about racial superiority and repatriation so that it constitutes part of a developed personal ideology, while the second is more akin to prejudice such as having pessimistic views about Afro-Caribbean learning potential. The first clearly has a structure while the second is mainly psychological. Institutional racism is a problematic notion that has been difficult to define, as the discussion later shows. Broadly, it is the claim that the practices and procedures that structure the way institutions operate in British society are racist because they take little or no account of its multiracial composition.

Confusingly, Swann also distinguishes between 'individual' racism and what it calls the 'climate' of racism, which is more pervasive and constitutes the ways in which the dominant procedures and practices in a society can reinforce and sustain institutional racism. Swann maintains that schools cannot assume neutrality when confronted by racism, but that their powers to change bedrock attitudes are limited by their role as socialization agencies. In line with its cultural pluralism, the stronger emphasis in Swann is on schools' reinterpreting the culture in multicultural terms: if education can reinforce what it means to be British in those terms its institutions will come to be trusted by the ethnic minorities, and social change by example and permeation rather than violence and force will be possible. However, this does not result in racism being eradicated. It is treated concurrently as a remediable social phenomenon, through such procedures as commissioning research, developing better statistics, and curricular proposals for multi-faith, religious education and mother-tongue maintenance. The report circles round the racism issue. Its definition of institutional racism could have provided the basis for a deeper examination of those structures in society that sustain and maintain racism, and anti-racism proposals might have stemmed from this. But this kind of analysis is limited by the committee's cultural-pluralistic rationale.

So far as teachers' expectations related to gender are concerned, there is a similar process of labelling and setting up self-fulfilling learning prophecies as the previous section on achievement and life chances suggests. To illustrate this, Clarricoates' (1980) research mentioned above, carried out in four primary schools in different socio-economic areas, studied the constructs of 'femininity' and 'masculinity' employed by teachers. She emphasizes (*ibid.* pp. 26–7) the immutability of these:

I hope to show that, despite the variations in sex-role stereotypes, it is not that some schools are less authoritarian or discriminatory to girls; rather the pattern, not the degree, of socialization changes to accommodate so-called 'liberal' attitudes to women. This could be defined as a 'divide and rule' philosophy.

One school was in a traditional working-class inner-city area, another suburban, another on a council estate and one was a village school. In each, teacher-instigated gender divisions that defined appropriate behaviour were detectable and were reinforced by the children's families. In Dockside, boys and girls were segregated inside and outside the school beginning in the reception class: separate playground, toilets, lines and registers. When asked whom they expected to do best, teachers characteristically replied in gender-related terms, such as 'Definitely the girls, but I think it's more to do with wanting to please rather than being intelligent'. Girls were also expected to set behaviour standards by being obedient and unaggressive. These divisions were also apparent in middle-class Applegate though they took the form of everyone being expected to be high achievers, with the boys being the highest and going on to university. This belief was reflected in the dominant family ethos of the husband being supported in his career by his non-working wife. If there was less sex segregation at Applegate it was because influences outside the school were maintaining this. Peer-group ridicule accepted and used tacitly by teachers was a powerful force for conformity: 'Two boys are happily playing in the Wendy House: Edward is setting the table while Tom is ironing. The teacher comes forward: "Aren't you busy? What are you playing?" Edward looks at Tom, both look sheepish. "Batman and Robin", states Edward vehemently. The teacher smiles and moves away' (*ibid.* p. 34). In Long Estate, sex segregation was less evident because of a progressive woman head, though staff attitudes revealed when confronted by 'deviant' behaviour were no less gender biased than in the other schools. The sex division of labour characterizing farming was strongly reflected in Linton Bray school even though girl pupils shared much of the arduous farm work with boys.

As for performance in a particular subject, Meighan (1986) cites mathematics as an example of girls' lower achievement being explained by biological factors. The reason why girls did less well at geometry problems was because they lacked 'spatial ability' that renders them 'unmathematical'. That this is due to lack of relevant experience is demonstrated by Sharma and Meighan's (1980) study in which girls and boys with similar experience did equally well in mathematics.

Finally, French (1986, p. 106) does not under-rate the difficulties of anti-sexist teaching:

> The overall situation is not, however, promising. Teachers can be made aware of the issues. They can monitor their lessons and perhaps identify subgroups of dominant pupils. They can also confront the possibility of their own sexism. But change also requires fundamental shifts in the attitudes of pupils. Girls would need, from the start, to acquire qualities of selfconfidence and assertion and to be less willing to accept or even endorse the behaviour of their male counterparts. And, importantly, they would not have to be made to feel by peers, parents, or teachers, less feminine as a consequence.
>
> Boys' notions of masculinity would likewise have to be challenged. The aura of arrogant self-confidence exuding from dominant boys would have to be dispelled. . . . In short, we would require a full-scale assault on society's gender consciousness.

The constraints on development, achievement and later life chances seem to outweigh the possibilities of working for race and gender equality according to some of the evidence here. Allied to this is the position of schools as State institutions committed to inducting the young into society and engaged in transmitting particular cultural messages in doing this. It would be easy to be deterministic about what might be seen to be the imperatives of human social development, and even more so when the implications of structural racism and sexism are dwelt upon. That the conditions in which equality goals are pursued are more complex than this should become clearer with the analysis of the equality concept and its operation in the next chapter.

3
SOCIAL JUSTICE AND EQUALITY

In this chapter the concept of equality as a practical moral principle applied to education is analysed. Its development is traced from its original meritocratic equal-opportunities interpretation and social-class basis to its different applications to race and gender equality, in order to develop the earlier referential framework concerning child-centredness for teachers engaged in equality policy-formation. Several aspects to do with teachers' decision-making in promoting equality are discussed and, in particular, the powerful affective factors involved.

Equality and Schooling: an Overview

The notion of equality related to State education can almost be seen as a by-product of educational provision. More tangible goals such as inculcating those skills and knowledge that an economically-effective workforce should have, and inducting the young into cherished values and mores, will necessarily be in the foreground of all State-funded education systems. For example, the DES paper, *The Curriculum from 5 to 16* (1985a), quotes six aims for primary and secondary schools that combine such qualities as promoting lively enquiring minds, physical skills, tolerance of other races, religions and ways of life with 'acquiring knowledge and skills relevant to adult life and employment in a fast changing world' (p. 3). The question of equality, in or through education, tends to apply once schooling becomes compulsory at a basic level such as that provided by the elementary system in Britain up to the 1940s, but optional and open to competition at the secondary level. This can be seen in the motives for developing elementary education in Britain beyond the Church-run voluntary societies' provisions that culminated in the Forster Education Act 1870. The economic arguments for extending schooling into the urban industrial areas, which the voluntary societies had inadequately penetrated, were at least as powerful as the social-reform motives. The awareness that Britain's industrial domination was being challenged by the USA, France and the newly-united Germany emphasized the need for a trained and educated workforce, while the increased franchise brought about by the Reform Bill 1867 required an electorate sufficiently educated to be able to understand and to accept the rights and duties of citizenship. Opportunities to go beyond basic, elementary, school provision inevitably arose because of the sheer number of children being educated in the new Board schools: the identification of talented children and the increasing technological requirements of industry demanded provision beyond the elementary school 'standards'. Thus, the so-called 'higher tops' or higher elementary schools in London and elsewhere provided a form of secondary education beyond school-leaving age, which was funded illegally by the School Boards. The Cockerton judgement of 1899, which successfully challenged this funding, halted this line of development.

The Education Act 1902 replaced the School Boards with local education authorities, which had jurisdiction over all State-funded education in their areas, including the new county-secondary schools that recruited mainly from elementary schools. With these schools and their competitive entry, the issue of equality of opportunity in education – together with the notion of a ladder of opportunity – came into fruition. The reasoning, therefore, was that while everyone (which meant, in fact, all children whose parents could not afford fees) had a right to an elementary education, only those children who successfully competed for a place had a right to a secondary education. This both accorded with and fulfilled the belief that only a small percentage of working-class children would be intelligent enough to benefit from a higher-level education, since the number of places available intensified competition. Darwinism was therefore vindicated and the middle-class stratum was rejuvenated by a steady flow of bright, working-class recruits.

The issue of egalitarianism – that everyone should have an equal education – arose with the claim that all should have equal access to a secondary education. In this view, equality and competition are inimical: the basic condition for providing equality in education is satisfied when there is equal right of access to it. But what pupils experience as education is a question beyond that of simple access. Should they be educated according to their defined abilities, needs and likely life chances, or should everyone have the same education? As the last chapter indicates, when deficit viewpoints prevail concerning girls' and ethnic-minority children's performance and potential, various inferior alternatives to high-status, mainstream education are likely to be recommended. Equal access is a necessary but not a sufficient condition and must be accompanied by an equal right to achieve, if equality of opportunity is to be realizable. Hence, the 1920s Labour-Party slogan of secondary education for all, to be implemented through a system of common schools. But the blueprint for the secondary system was established by the tripartite doctrine of the three major pre-war reports, Hadow, Spens and Norwood, which took the apparently child-centred viewpoint that pupils should be educated according to their diagnosed needs and abilities. Because all of the reports lacked a developed social dimension, their provisions for secondary schooling were a projection partly of beliefs about the measurability of potential, and partly of the class structure – obscured by the doctrine of parity of esteem between the proposed three types of school.

What was implemented, therefore, reverted back to Tawney's 'tadpole philosophy' of the beginning of the century: many tadpoles are needed in order to produce a few frogs. This was a re-affirmation of élitism justified scientifically by the use of psychometric instruments to identify educational potential. An overarching condition was the continued economic slump in the 1930s, which allowed some expansion of the existing system, so that by 1939 about 65 per cent of the school population were receiving a secondary education. The Education Act 1944 confirmed tripartism within the notion of primary and secondary stages in education.

The 1950s and 1960s were marked by a resurgence of the equal opportunity to achieve interpretation underpinned by the rise of sociological research and the relative decline of psychological enquiry, which examined issues such as social class and family influences on educability, the effects of streaming, class-related language codes, the phenomenon of 'cultural' deprivation and community schooling. All took educability and school achievement as their main focal point. Colemen's concern with compensatory education programmes in the USA in the 1960s led him to define equality of opportunity as the equal right to achieve in school.

The debate pointed to the need for children to have access to the same educational experience, and the need, therefore, for common schools with an undifferentiated entry, mixed ability or delayed-ability grouping, and a common curriculum, at least until school-leaving age. The bilateral schools of the 1930s were a step towards the comprehensive principle, but taken for economic rather than egalitarian reasons. In the 1940s and 1950s several small authorities reorganized along comprehensive lines, again for economic reasons but some larger urban ones such as London opened purpose-built comprehensives as an expression of socialist egalitarianism, and more specifically, to combat the negative self-fulfilling prophecies set up when children were allocated to secondary-modern schools as a result of 'failing' the 11-plus selection tests. These schools, therefore, represented limited attempts at social engineering, whereby children across the social class and ability range would be educated in the one school, but where the normal, internal, organization pattern based on ability grouping actually segregated them into streams and sets. It was not until the 1960s that the self-fulfilling prophecy effects of streaming, in particular, were disseminated through a major NFER study and several smaller ones, and the trend towards mixed-ability grouping began.

Again, largely for economic and efficiency rather than egalitarian reasons, curricular commonality or at least the power to exercise some direct control over curricular provision has been a central-government concern since the 1860s. From then, up to 1926, the State curriculum was in practice defined by the yearly elementary school *Codes* published by the Board of Education. In 1926 these were abolished by a Conservative government facing defeat by the Labour opposition as a political move intended to block Labour's intention to establish a universal secondary system in common schools, as White (1975) has documented. From this point, curricular jurisdiction passed to the local authorities who generally delegated their responsibilities to the schools. The commality issue resurfaced in 1976 with Callaghan's Ruskin College speech initiating the so-called Great Debate. The range of discussion and policy formation papers published by the HMI and the DES between 1977 and 1985 were all primarily concerned with defining a common curriculum to serve a combination of personal-education, economic-efficiency and social-justice aims. The HMI papers were clearly grounded in current educational theory concerning the nature of knowledge in that they developed a Hirstian disciplines-based approach – almost an education for its own sake view – but the approach taken in the DES papers during this period was a more tightly-articulated version of the status quo, being conventional subjects-based, more hard-line on standards and concerned with promoting an educational-efficiency view of schooling. This, of course, is the view that prevailed in the centrally- directed curricular clauses in the 1988 Act.

It is clear that inequality in education has been and still is related both structurally and psychologically to being working class; Jeffcoate (1984) goes further in claiming that class rather than race factors are crucial when considering ethnic-minority group inequalities. But, with the emergence of the twin issues of race and gender equality, following the Race Relations Act 1976 and the Sex Discrimination Act 1975, the debate linking social-class membership, educability and achievement and equality has become more of a set of underlying concerns used by some educationists to emphasize the structural nature of race and sex inequalities. Somewhat behind these issues in public awareness, the arguments extending educational equality to disabled children, focusing on their integration into mainstream education following the Warnock Report and the Education Act 1981, has also drawn attention to a particular category of children.

Analysing the Concept

Equality is essentially a practical principle that has everything to do with rights being established over the fair distribution of valued resources. Warnock (1977) points out its reliance on political decision-making: whereas the conviction that there ought to be fair shares is rooted in natural justice and personal moral codes, in a society the rule that this shall be so depends on a practical political decision being made. But while the rule establishes the basic right, it does not stipulate what will be fair. This is important when the principle is applied to education:

> there is a difference between claiming that everyone has an equal right to education and saying that everyone has a right to equal education. In order to claim either of these rights it is necessary that there should be a law. But the law under which the second claim could be made would be a great deal more specific than the law under which the first could be made.
>
> (*Ibid*. p. 26)

While the first makes the basic claim that everyone has an equal right to be educated, the second is problematic since it raises the egalitarian question of what counts as an equal education. Does it mean that everyone should have exactly the same education? Or access to a number of educational experiences that are equivalent to each other? Or an education that is different in experiences, quantity and demands and justified on the grounds that it is appropriate to the different needs and capabilities of different children? The last question raises the subsidiary ones of who decides this, with what authority and on what grounds?

What is involved here are two accounts of the operation of equality: these are the flat, equalitarian viewpoint or the equal-shares viewpoint, in which everyone is judged to have the same rights regarding their membership of a society. That is, in the eyes of the law they are considered to be equal and the same because each is a human being – since people share similar characteristics, they merit the same treatment so that their needs can be met. The second account, or distributive-justice viewpoint, argues that equality is achieved when the differences between individuals are recognized and the resources they have an equal right to are allocated on the grounds of these differences. Succinctly, it entails that equals be treated equally, and unequals unequally. As Warnock points out, it is crucial in the distributive-justice position that there is a principle established that can be applied in order to justify different treatment on the grounds of different characteristics, otherwise children could be subjected to the whims and *ad hoc* judgements of those in authority over them. Justification is the major difficulty: what will count as the main reason for treating some pupils differently from others? Research evidence, teachers' beliefs and expectations or local authority ideologies? Are these different qualities and characteristics real or the projections of ideological beliefs? In schools with multiracial intakes, those teachers who maintain a colour-blind stance justify this in support of their view that all children have much the same educational needs; they would claim that to discriminate in favour of some by giving them different treatment is misguided and unfair. So are there real differences that can be demonstrated objectively, perhaps by research findings, and that would justify different learning experiences and resources harnessed to the same educational goals? This, of course, is the basis for positive-discrimination approaches, but it still leaves unanswered the question of how to justify which learning experiences. For example, there would appear to be no objections at the practical level to equipping children whose mother tongue is not English to achieve in British schools by teaching them English. But there is the more-complex, less-immediately practical question of what happens to their cultural and racial identities if their mother tongue is not also developed. Perhaps this can be answered by the claim that reducing children to pupildom is contrary to education and personal development, but this provokes further questions as to the proper roles and purposes of schools, teachers and pupils.

A more extended example might illustrate the difficulties by considering what a teacher might do when confronted by them. Supposing that in an infants' class the Lego is monopolized by the boys, with the girls showing little interest in it: what should the teacher do? If the boys continue to monopolize the Lego because the teacher simply makes it available, she could justify this on the grounds of boys' and girls' natural characteristics and interests, since it is open to anyone to use it. If the teacher believes that the girls' mechanical skills are poorer than the boys' because of lack of experience, she will be justified in making a number of escalating responses depending on the centrality or otherwise of her views on the matter – persuading some girls to use it, or making Lego a girls-only activity for part of the day, or making it a daily compulsory activity for girls. More obliquely, motivated by a belief and a deeper understanding of structural gender inequalities, the teacher could work to make the girls assertive and confident enough to intervene by themselves and to make the boys more sensitive to others' rights and needs. Behind these decisions is the reasoning that the girls' lack of a skill is not a natural phenomenon but the result of their chosen or forced lack of experience in a particular activity. At this point, the teacher has to decide how important this deficiency is for the girls' progress.

It is also at this point that observable events, such as the boys' superiority in mechanical skills, become connected to values positions, such as the right for boys and girls in her class to achieve equally. If the teacher considers that the lack of such skills impedes the girls from achieving equally with boys, she will intervene. If the teacher's values position applies mainly to her classroom and the children she teaches or, to a situation over which the teacher has considerable direct control and influence, she is likely to take equal opportunities to achieve as her main aim. If the teacher's perspectives reach beyond the classroom and school, she is likely to have a reasoned standpoint on sex-equitable or anti-sexist education and to see the classroom more directly in terms of women's life chances and women's roles in society. What is crucial here, therefore, is the teacher's personal and professional ideology by which her classroom decisions are justified. It will be the teacher's professional concern to consider the accounts and the evidence in order to decide what if anything she needs to do.

Another example can be used to illustrate the errors that can result from basing strategies on misleading or ill-considered evidence. A combination of the distributive-justice principle and the belief in the fixed, inherited nature of children's abilities has been used to justify streaming and subject-setting in secondary, and ability-grouping in primary, schools. The reasoning is that individual learning will be improved if the ability range in a group is narrow: teachers will be better able to match their planning and resourcing to the different ability levels of the separate groups. There tend to be arbitrary factors built into all these forms of grouping dictated by organizational constraints. In ability-grouped primary classrooms, for instance, the number of groups is likely to be determined as much or more by the room size, number of children, type and amount of furniture and learning resources than the ability spread. Why six groups in one class and four in another? The means by which abilities are assessed are unlikely to be precise enough to allow clear cut-off points between the groups, so there will be overlaps. It is also likely that the groups will be based on a single indicator such as reading ability, but that children will stay in them for all learning activities. The children themselves will be very clear about their group's position in the class hierarchy and what is expected from them, and it will be no surprise to the teacher that the groups' composition remains about the same throughout the year. So what is implemented to improve achievement and promote equality thereby in fact operates against these goals.

It can be seen that the question of equal rights to an education – that is, equality of access – is quickly superceded by the question of the equal right to achieve, once the issue of who should receive what sort of education is addressed. The claim here is that it makes no sense to talk about equal access without also talking about equality of opportunity defined as school achievement, since at the point when a child enters school, he or she is subject to the schools' aims and objectives, all or most of which concern achievement in academic, personal, expressive and social terms. This is the issue behind Crosland's (1962) argument that there is a strong and a weak interpretation of equality at work in the education system. In the weak sense, there is equality of access to high-status academic education in that competition to get places in grammar schools (at that time) is technically open to all pupils. However, such access is limited in that it only applies to State schools. It is qualified by the existence of higher-status, fee-paying public schools. Also, access is further compromised by being very much on a social-class basis with middle-class pupils predominating in grammar schools. Many of the small proportion of working-class entrants tended to do less well or to leave early, thus 'proving' that working-class children were less intelligent than middle-class children. This is what he was really attacking: the belief in the inherited, unchanging nature of intelligence that was ostensibly demonstrated by the nature of the grammar-school entry.

His argument for a strong interpretation of equality is based on his dismissal of the innate-intelligence view and his counter-claim that every child has a right to acquire intelligence in the school system. The conditions for bringing this about would entail eliminating economic-deprivation factors such as low incomes and poor housing, which demonstrably affect school achievement. If these artificial barriers to performance were removed and the education system better resourced, the strong interpretation of equality of opportunity could be implemented. His reconceptualizing of the notion of achievement follows from his dismissal of the view that academic achievement is based on inherited intelligence. His third interpretation of equality – the strongest of all definitions – required children to have equal chances to develop their personalities and interests to achieve self-fulfilment as well as that of being able to contribute to the economy as members of an educated workforce.

Coleman's argument, mentioned earlier and located in the American education system in the 1960s, takes a similar line. He distinguishes between several stages of development of the equal opportunities concept: the first concerns equal access, in which all children have an actual right to schooling, with the potential right to succeed at it. The second concerns this output, and the effects schooling has on different children; he contends that instead of schooling being a race in which there are many losers, schools should take the initiative in developing educational success by formulating goals that are achievable by all. He therefore rejects the meritocratic belief that education should be competitive, which sees it as a resource, a commodity bargained for in the striving for upward mobility. Warnock (1977, p. 41) also rejects what she describes as the opportunity to compete, which combines two in-combatible theories: 'For it seems now to be the height of disingenuous-ness to combine the theory of competition, a theory which quite openly admits that there is a prize to be won by the competitors, with the theory that everyone is going to be provided with something according to his need'.

But is competition intrinsic to equality of opportunity? Eradicating competition by widening the basis of school achievement to admit all could cause agencies outside schools to reject or devalue what the schools are producing. The effect of this would be to re-assert the worth of traditional forms of school achievement gained through competition. Is Coleman's anti-competition viewpoint no more than an educational myth, therefore, in which schools have the power to determine their own learning goals and what counts as achievement regardless of the way that the forces outside schools define this? Crosland, Coleman and Warnock raise central questions especially concerning the purposes of State-funded education. Broadly, is the view that education should be 'pure' – that is, geared to individual growth – bound to be in conflict with the view that education should be 'applied', or a means to other ends in a society, where those ends are attained either by competition or ascription? Crosland's strongest-of-all interpretations of equality is actually a return to the flat, equalitarian approach, in which equality is achieved by everyone being treated in the same way. Competition could be abolished in a fully-common schooling system, but the question of the credibility of its output outside the schools would still depend on who had the power to define school achievement, a factor that might challenge the Hargreaves/Thomas reconceptualized four aspects of achievement, for instance.

Also, there is still the argument that downgrading competition inevitably means abandoning the field of academic high-status education for doubtful alternatives such as achievement in non-academic and low-status areas, sports and expressive arts, or Stone's (1981) MRE. Attempts at this in the State system have persuaded Afro-Caribbean groups to set up sup-plementary schools whose purpose is to reinstate mainstream learning.

The power to define the nature of achievement residing in institutions outside schools also carries with it the power to define its ceiling. If the system was effective enough to produce a large number of leavers with high qualifications, this would not in itself produce equality because of structural inequalities in the labour market. Bash, Coulby and Jones (1985, p. 136) claim that

> The *stratification of the labour market* is such that public and private employers actually require young people with different skills at different levels. Industry, commerce, the professions and service facilities need some young people with a high level of specific specialised skill. They also need people with low-level skills or virtually no skills at all. If schools do not produce unskilled and unqualified young people, then they will fail to meet one of the demands of the labour market.

They go on to argue that if schools did produce equally-achieving pupils, employers would apply their own tests in order to fit recruits into the hierarchy of jobs available. If this is so, the implications are far-reaching: that the labour market, because of its stratification, determines the nature of school achievement and, ultimately, what counts as education.

Liberal and Radical Perspectives on Equality

These two opposed perspectives will be outlined in order to draw the political parameters of the equality debate. They are presented more as ideal types than working ideologies. The liberal, consensual viewpoint is located and is meaningful in a democratic society; it claims that although serious inequalities exist, these can be reduced or minimized by improving socio-economic conditions and public services such as education through the exercise of democratic government. It is, therefore, evolutionary. By constant improvements to the status quo, the position of the disadvantaged in society can be raised so that they can compete on equal terms with others. Education is seen very much in terms of sponsoring social mobility through equality of opportunity. The paradox of equality being defined as meritocratic is countered by the argument that if a growing number of people improve their status and economic situation through high achievement in school, this increases the amount of equality in society.

In outline, the radical, conflictual perspective claims that oppression is built into the structure of democratic societies through their class systems. The role of schooling is to categorize people to fit defined, subordinate roles in the capitalist system. Power is exerted by the ruling group in defining what counts as school knowledge, which groups will have access to what kinds and qualities of knowledge and how achievement is to be defined and assessed. In this perspective, there is no equality; its absence can be masked by child-centred methods in schools that make schooling more palatable. Attempts to produce it through positive-discrimination strategies, for example, are a sham and do no more than acknowledge the existing power structure since they produce no structural change. Thus, the radical perspective directly invokes the power issue in society: what upward mobility there is, is anti-equality since it is geared to regenerating the ruling group, the class structure and capitalism.

Either stance would present problems to a group of teachers trying to use it as a conceptual structure for an equality policy. One renders equality meaningless by denying its possibility; the other sees it as a product of educational success within an unchanged political system in which the problems of competition and merit largely remain unaddressed. Both ascribe an inherently limited, static role to schools as perpetuators of dominant social values. The liberal view sees this as initiating the young into dominant values and equipping them with the skills needed for them to become viable adults, while the radical view sees it as the means by which the young are processed for roles in an exploitative society.

The two perspectives do provide a general referential framework in which teachers can locate their own views on equality, and particularly their feelings about unfairness and injustice, in the process of developing some principles for practical action. In the case of equality issues and practices, such feelings make the abstract principles and injunctions mean something important in terms of individual children. Macro-statements such as the two perspectives are hardly meant to be focused down to micro-situations like schools and classrooms since they are accounts of general forces and conflicts operating in society.

So, how do people arrive at decisions to act? A more 'natural' way begins with the concrete and moves towards the abstract as justification, in starting with known quantities, such as the people for whom one has some responsibility who are disadvantaged; to move from their predicament to some general explanations, and then to consider what must be done. For teachers, this will be more than a matter of charity, since the people concerned will be children in their own classrooms. So, what is being argued is that people arrive at decisions that invariably originate and gain their impetus from a conviction that someone they are responsible for is being subjected to unfair or unjust treatment or conditions. Such decisions will be capable of being justified rationally by looking at the evidence and relating it to general principles, and so on. The crucial condition is that such treatment challenges their personal and professional values. It is also disinterested action: the actor does not benefit. It is not, for instance, a matter of carrying out a remedial task instrumentally to achieve certain goals such as trying to increase social and economic efficiency through improving achievement in schools. When people care about promoting equality they are exercising moral views about the non-development of individual talent, the reduction of individual worth and the impoverishment of individual lives as a consequence – and trying to do what is in their power to ameliorate these.

The affective, empathetic factor in equality decision-making is powerful and not to be denied, as Warnock (1977, p. 54) argues:

> Although it is nice to seem concerned and to appear to care for men as one's brothers, there is also a stigma attached to paternalism; and compassion is akin to charity, often thought of as the virtue most studiously to be avoided. But was the motive force behind the positive discrimination arguments, for instance, really a passion for equality? I doubt it. It seems far more likely that it was mostly a sense of outrage and of pity that any children should have to live and grow up in such hopeless situations.

She suggests also that compassion was the motive behind Crosland's and Tawney's promotion of equality.

The practice of equality, like the practice of other key, moral principles (such as promoting individual liberty) is not tidy-minded, therefore; the abstract procedural principles that provide their structure have to be cashed in individual terms, as a first step to formulating actions and programmes. Teachers' responses are unlikely to be couched in the pure terms of the opposing perspectives. If the liberal, consensual perspective seems difficult to apply because it relies too much on the assumed rational acts of rational beings who are all basically in agreement, the conflictual perspective provides the Gordian knot solution, apparently – belief in inherent superiority leading to oppression expresses the structural realities of capitalism and remedies can only come from radical changes to that structure. While they provide explanations – within a particular ideological framework – concerning the location of power, the nature of oppression, disinterested action and such like, the personal factors, the essential inconsistencies, the 'how' questions come to be formulated when their claims are filtered through teachers' own ideologies. The fact that these are by their nature embedded in teachers' practices and are hardly meant to be articulated suggests that the first phase of equality policy decision-making in a school will succeed only if the climate supports open debate among a staff so that differences can be made explicit and agreement on how to proceed can be reached.

Equality, Merit and Multicultural Education

Crosland's (1962) strongest interpretation of equality tried to set aside the narrower notion of equal rights to achieve academically in favour of asserting that every child should have an equal right to developing his or her interests and personality 'regardless of measured intelligence'. This child-centred view of the role of education is concerned with individual development and autonomy and eschews competition for academic goals. Similarly, Jeffcoate (1984) attacks equality of opportunity for being meritocratic rather than egalitarian, and asks why successful school learning in the expressive arts or games should not be valued as highly as academic achievement. Warnock asserts the status quo in claiming that nothing can eliminate the high value of academic achievement or the competition it engenders because there are ineradicable inequalities in jobs and roles in all societies. She therefore confirms the points made from a different political perspective by Bash, Coulby and Jones about structural inequalities in British society. How might such views help teachers engaged in equality policy-making?

As argued, their views will be shaped by a combination of their political, moral and educational beliefs and what they perceive as unfairness and inequality experienced by their pupils, inside and outside the school. Their main criteria for action are likely to be identified by questions such as, 'What should I do in the best interests of my pupils?' and 'What is possible, given available resources and expertise?' In a multiracial primary school, the reasoning might be that if children's experience is to be the basis of their education, the content of the curriculum for all children should reflect the racial composition of British society.

The origins, interpretations and development of multicultural education, or Gaine's (1987) 'racial education' are a mixture of official government initiatives and teachers' and other educationists' frequently-conflicting viewpoints. Arguably, multicultural/racial education has been compromised from its beginnings because responses from the early assimilationist preoccupation with instilling good English onwards, have been conceived in terms of actual and assumed differences between ethnic-minority and white children rather than as a valid educational experience for all children.

The concept developed through strategies to cope in the schools with the children of black immigrants during the mass-migration period up until the 1960s, followed by the gradual recognition that ethnic-minority groups were expanding the cultural dimensions of British society, which culminated in the notion of society itself being multicultural. The development can therefore be seen in terms of the official stances that shaped the educational responses: assimilation, integration and cultural pluralism or, from the belief that immigrants should be absorbed into the indigenous culture, to a conditional but increasingly liberal acceptance of cultural diversity.

The assimilationist model asserted the importance of national unity;

immigrants should become British as soon as possible, culturally and politically. The problem, as Mullard (1982) points out, concerns what is the 'British' way of life. It is impossible to talk about shared values, attitudes and behaviours unless the hierarchical nature of British society is also acknowledged. The major educational aim of assimilationism was the inculcation of standard English, frequently through segregating immigrant children in language centres and feeding them back into normal schools when their English was judged competent. Thus, through a positive-discrimination strategy they were equipped to succeed in the educational mainstream. Some justification for this approach came from those immigrant parents who had come here as much to acquire educational life chances for their children as to obtain regular jobs for themselves. Critics such as Mullard claim that indoctrination and social conditioning underlay the apparently instrumental goals of language acquisition: that from a position of disadvantage, with their own culture rejected, they were not expected to prosper in the education system or to compete successfully with white peers for good jobs.

The integrationist model is more liberal and rejects the implicit racism of assimilationism. It is epitomized in Roy Jenkins' often-quoted words as Home Secretary in the mid-1960s as 'not a flattening process of assimilation but equal opportunity, accompanied by cultural diversity, in an atmosphere of mutual tolerance'. While English remained important, an equalizing process would develop by representing the cultures of ethnic minorities in the curriculum. At face value, the principle is liberal but the continued implicit supremacy of the indigenous culture means that integration cannot be on equal terms. If a permeation approach is used there is the danger of tokenism – an amalgam of curious customs, exotic food and clothes stands in for the minority culture. If multicultural education is a separate activity, by definition it is outside the mainstream and an inferior alternative to it. From the point of view of life chances, integrationism is not much more than a liberal form of assimilation since basic cultural inequalities are not challenged within it.

Cultural pluralism, on the other hand, celebrates difference. Mullard claims that this model is a refined version of the earlier two, in which the idea of cultural diversity is made central. Because of its relativity principle it represents a stronger approach to equality than integrationism. It is more likely to define particular educational needs such as mother-tongue maintenance in terms of a culture's intrinsic value and its potential to contribute to the cultural mosaic of Britain than as a learning deficit.

There are two major criticisms of multicultural education: first, that it plays down or ignores the distribution of power in British society. Mullard

(1982, p. 130) claims that 'it is patently clear that black groups in a white society, black pupils in white schools, could not develop their cultural traditions without the unconditional permission, approval and encouragement of white society as a whole and of white dominant power groups in particular'. This suggests that any attempt at multicultural education is compromised from the beginning since it operates from a deficit position – lack of political and economic power defines ethnic-minority groups as being also culturally disadvantaged. Therefore it is essentially compensatory education for a depressed minority and beset with the same deficit-learning perspectives for which its 1960s educational priority area (EPA) class-based predecessor was attacked.

The second criticism concerns minority pupils' access to education: if something described as multicultural education is provided for them – and this is its basic flaw – as a response to their diagnosed needs, this excludes them from the mainstream, with its access to high-status knowledge, achievement recognized through public examinations and consequent highly-valued employment. Stone (1981) attacked a multiracial education or MRE, which Gaine (1987) describes as an earlier form of multicultural education and as being a response to a claimed major influence on black children's school performance, their depressed self-images. She argued that the intended therapy of MRE exacerbated the problem because it offered black children an inferior substitute for real education. If the link between self-image and achievement is taken to be problematic, then one of two conclusions can be drawn. Moderate critics might say that MRE is acting in good faith but is based on a false analysis; radical ones would claim it is an instrument for continuing black oppression. The first would acknowledge that equality aims are being pursued through defective positive-discrimination premises and strategies, the second would deny the possibility of equality for blacks in a white, middle-class dominated society.

What are at the heart of both criticisms are the claims that British society is racist, that plurality is an illusion and that multicultural education expresses how the power structure operates and is an attempt to impose it through indoctrination and social control. To an extent, these are evidenced by the Swann Committee in its limited consideration of institutional and personal racism and its avoidance of the power issue, in its pursuit of 'education for all'. This stance also represented the art of the possible for a committee trying to arrive at realistic recommendations for right-wing, central-government policy-making. If the criticisms are upheld, the position of equal opportunities for ethnic-minority children within a multicultural education setting is a matter of assimilation to the indigenous white culture and therefore depends on individual merit.

The criticisms also go some way towards explaining why multiculturalism has been challenged by various forms of anti-racism. Gaine (1987), after Hatcher, describes these as 'weak' or education for racial equality (ERE), and 'strong' or anti-racist education (ARE), which makes the connection with social class. The class-membership difference is crucial, since while the first, or ERE, claims that racism is a social evil that can be countered, and that makes some form of 'strong' multicultural education possible, the second, or ARE, makes the essentially Marxist point that racism, with classism, is structural. Anti-racist education, therefore, has a structural location and is 'a black response to white racism' (*ibid.* p. 36), whereas education for racial equality, because of its cultural-phenomenon view of racism, is simply a more radical version of multicultural education that takes racism as an evil to be remedied. In fact, the division is not clear-cut, since many expressions of ERE take a structural view of racism but do not proceed to make the Marxist deductions from it, as the discussion of the ILEA equality policies in Chapter 4 indicates. It is ERE that informs the policy-making of local authorities such as Berkshire and ILEA and virtually all the examples of school-based policies discussed in Chapters 6 and 7, though Gayhurst Infants', with its emphasis on community involvement and action, does take more of an ARE stand. Its strongest educational attribute is that it confronts the question, 'Who is it really for?' Multicultural education with its definition of educational needs in ethnic-minority, cultural-characteristics terms arguably was 'for' ethnic-minority children, usually implicitly. ARE is also 'for' ethnic-minority children because of its location in minority groups' oppression. Education for racial equality is 'for' all children since it seeks to counter racism that it locates in white social groups:

> So ERE would claim to want to give pupils a critical understanding of racism rather than hope for 'harmony' through goodwill, and it seeks to rethink structures and practices which diminish life-chances for black people. In practice this means, for instance, positive action on black recruitment, monitoring job appointments and being prepared to act upon the results, and having enforceable sanctions for racists at any level.
>
> (Gaine, 1987, pp. 34–5)

As Gaine points out, there are clear messages here concerning relevance and immediacy for pupils and teachers in all-white as well as racially-mixed schools, which cannot be claimed for multicultural education.

If the furthering of equality is seen as a process taking place within the present political and economic structure, education for racial equality is potentially the central, mainstream educational experience, and arguably the most radical stance that political power groups in central government and local authorities would be likely to accept. The recent plan by a Conservative authority to abolish Berkshire's anti-racism policy and its withdrawal as a result of local action is only one indication of a shift to the right in race matters, so even this is debatable. ERE could be the most effective means for achieving the kind of black social mobility together with the development of a substantial economically-influential, black middle class of the kind that is evolving in the USA as the route to equality in a class-based society. This would entail that social mobility is not only in terms of black recruitment to the caring professions such as teaching and social work, but that there will also be a sizeable representation in front-line economic jobs such as managing banks, insurance companies and building societies and in the higher executive reaches of large firms. Since the capitalist system in Britain does not show too many signs yet of collapsing upon its own contradictions, the traditional mode of social ascent – beset as it is by competition and charges of meritocracy – could be argued to be the most realistic as distinct from idealistic approach to developing some form of race equality.

Equality and Gender in Education

Because of the embeddedness of gender issues and the lack of official stances compared with those on race, the processes that might connect girls' access to education, achievement and equality are less clear-cut. There has been nothing like the gradation of central-government and local-authority responses as with race, as Arnot (1987, p. 320) observes:

> It is significant that no explicit policy statement has been issued by the DES concerning equal opportunities for girls/women. A policy statement on sex equality would be even less likely, given the current political climate. Further, there has been no committee of enquiry to examine sex inequality comparable to the Rampton/Swann Committee investigating racial disadvantage in education. No central funds have been allocated to cater for the needs of girls along the lines of Section 11 grants for schools with a high proportion of ethnic minority pupils, nor has the DES prioritized gender as a concern for in-service funding. The DES has selected a role which one could argue is minimal and non-interventionist.

She claims that the only direct DES involvement in sex-equality promotion has been through a few in-service training courses on aspects of sex-stereotyping and developing equal opportunities in schools; there is very little in the major reports and policy papers, though she points out that the CATE criteria for initial teacher-training include possible sex-equality initiatives.

Table 3.1 Gender issues in schooling

Laissez-faire (traditional)	*Laissez-faire* (contemporary)	Sex equitable/ egalitarian	Anti-sexist	Feminist
Education according to natural boy/girl differences viewpoint on abilities, interests, aptitudes. Separate boy/girl schooling	Natural differences viewpoint modified by individual differences ideology: child-centredness. Co-education for social development	Belief that boy/girl differences are largely cultural. Notion of equal opportunity of access/achievement becomes a guiding principle. Separate or co-education	Strong belief in individual differences: explicit anti-natural differences. Equal opportunities through equalizing boy/girl power in school	Education based on belief in structural male power, female oppression. Education necessarily separate
Power dimension given, non-problematic. School and society contexts	Power dimension still largely unproblematic. Seen in terms of relations in school: not seen in societal terms	Power dimension becoming problematic in personal individual terms: providing girls with better opportunities can remedy unfairness. Societal dimension acknowledged as background influence	Power dimension as structural as well as personal. School context seen as projection of power distribution in society	Structural power distinctive of patriachal society. Impossibility of sex equality because of power distribution
Curriculum: boy/girl subjects selection as expression of natural differences. Knowledge seen as neutral	Curriculum: recognition of individual abilities, interests cutting across sex membership, but still 'natural' self-selection. Knowledge as neutral	Curriculum: access as key to achievement, so some guiding of choice: 'weak' positive discrimination. Knowledge as synthetically male-biased	Curriculum: 'strong' positive discrimination in combating male domination of high-status subjects. Knowledge as male-dominated: expression of power distribution, but this can be combated in schools	Curriculum: subjects recast in women's terms to redefine school knowledge

In the absence of an official policy, a number of viewpoints on sex equality and education in rough historical order can be portrayed, with the understanding that they all still exist (see Table 3.1). The last three in particular correspond with policy views on race. Comparisons can be made according to how each of them deals with the issue of power operating in a society. So, sex equity resembles the cultural, pluralist, multicultural-education approach in that unequal educational performance and life chances are seen to result from girls' lack of the opportunity to achieve in boy-dominated high-status areas of the curriculum rather than influenced by the way power is distributed and exercised in society. The solutions proposed are forms of positive discrimination in which girls are given better access to learning materials and bodies of knowledge traditionally dominated by boys. In primary schools, topics and projects would express cross-gender interests rather than favouring the boys; teachers would be more aware of the effects of sex-stereotyping, and would try to counter it by redistributing children's classroom tasks and roles.

An anti-sexist stance corresponds with the weak form of anti-racism – Gaine's ERE. The examples of schools' anti-sexism policies in Chapter 6 follow this 'weak' version. As with education for racial equality, male power is perceived as an institutional feature of society. School and teacher intervention therefore challenges this power distribution by consciously trying to alter the roles, expectations and educational experiences of girls inside and outside classrooms in order to raise their achievement levels in traditionally boy-dominated areas of knowledge. This might be little more than the extra-access approach associated with sex equity, but a more developed version – for example, that of ILEA – would also try to make boys more caring and able to express their emotions and girls more assertive and confident so that their bids for more power, at least in the school setting, would be both successful and sustained. By making more girls educationally successful – according to male-defined terms – it should be possible to equip women to compete with men for prestigious jobs and roles in society that are the means by which power is acquired and eventually equalized. The parallel here is with the development of an economically-powerful black middle class.

The feminist stance is as radical as 'strong' anti-racism in its location in women's oppression rather than classroom practices and its claim that power is structural and patriarchal. A major claim is that girls need to be educated separately from boys because it is not possible to challenge male dominance effectively in a mixed setting. This is an expression of a central feminist belief, that males and females inhabit different emotional worlds that makes equal co-existence the only achievable possibility since their different and separate states excludes mutual understanding. In this it is very like the exclusivity of ARE.

The analysis suggests that while all of the perspectives on race and gender equality are problematic in development and operation, the more moderate ones have attained a degree of acceptance among local authorities and concerned teachers involved in equality policy-making. Thus, anti-racism in its weak sense and the cultural-pluralist multicultural approach typify most local authority initiatives. Similarly, sex equality and moderate forms of anti-sexism have been adopted by the smaller number of authorities that take sex equally to be as important as race equality.

4
EQUALITY POLICY-MAKING: LOCAL-AUTHORITY INITIATIVES

Two local-authority equal-opportunity policies are contrasted, the radical ILEA anti-racist and sexist, and the moderate Kent statement in which a sex-equitable approach is central. These two also have markedly different implementation styles in which schools and teachers are expected to play very different innovation roles. It is argued that a school-based innovation approach, in contrast to top-down strategies, is more likely to lead to workable equality policies being implemented.

The Nature of the Policies

Equality policies have been produced by about half the local education authorities in Britain. Many of the urban ones have concentrated on promoting race equality through an anti-racist approach, while others such as Kent have produced moderate statements opposing discrimination on the grounds of sex, race and disabilities. Styles of implementation also range between the tightly-organized, top-down, from country hall, to the schools approaches of inner-city authorities such as Ealing, Brent, Haringay and ILEA, and the recommendatory guidelines for good-practice approach adopted by Kent.

In most of the inner-cities authorities, and other pioneering ones such as Berkshire, the orientation has been anti-racist of the 'weak', education-for-racial-equality type in Gaine's (1987) terms. In some policies, such as ILEA's, the cultural-pluralist, multicultural-education approach is explicitly rejected because of its inadequacies in combating racism. Typically, these policies advocate anti-racist teaching strategies as being necessary and prior to developing multi-ethnic education: the reasoning is that it is not possible to reconceptualize school knowledge in multi-ethnic terms until the fact of racism in the schools is confronted. Therefore, behaviour ranging from racialist abuse and attacks, to unconscious expressions of prejudice, have to be opposed by teachers in pursuing their normal duties, whether the offender is a pupil, parent, ancillary worker or another teacher. In this approach, teachers' anti-racist attitudes and actions are taken to be the mainsprings for change; curriculum rebuilding and resources appraisal and renewal take place in a school ethos permeated by anti-racism.

Like any radical proposal for change, the approach has its critics. There are two separate problematic areas: the question of racism both as a social phenomenon and a structural feature of British society; and the styles of policy implementation adopted by local authorities. The first, as expressed by critics such as Jeffcoate (1984), questions the validity of the concept of institutional racism that underpins anti-racist approaches. He distinguishes between four senses or types of racism: first, as a set of beliefs rooted in physical appearances; second, in the form of prejudices and stereotypes held by individuals against groups; third, attacks and other acts of discrimination, often termed racialism; and, fourth, what has been termed institutional racism. While he argues the first three are unambiguous because they are observable in their different ways as social phenomena, the fourth is problematic to him:

> Its shortcomings as a tool of analysis in the field of education are only too apparent. Whereas it is relatively clear how 'scientific' and 'popular' racism might manifest themselves in schools – in the attitudes and behaviour of teachers and pupils, in the curriculum and other aspects of school policy – what institutional racism refers to remains as obscure as in other spheres.
>
> (*Ibid.* p. 145)

He particularly takes issue with ILEA's definition because of the general-ized impression of black people's position in society on which it is based, and the practice of using institutional racism as a catch-all explanation for race inequalities. This is a crucial criticism because institutional racism is taken by ILEA as being the mainspring for personal/behavioural racism, or Jeffcoate's three valid types. It is the main organizing concept, therefore, in anti-racist policies; if doubts can be cast about its existence, the policy's validity is threatened. Some of the examples Jeffcoate gives to illustrate its analytical inadequacies include the tendency to attribute black under-achievement to institutional racism, as if this is sufficient explanation. He takes issue with the way it has been used 'to refer to just about anything in the education system the writer or speaker happens to dislike' (*ibid*. p. 146); for example, he claims, ethnocentricity in the curriculum, rather than being racist, is more likely to be a manifestation of teacher ignorance and parochialism.

The Runnymeade Trust's (1985, p. 5) summary of the Swann Report echoes the problems of definition but less critically:

> The term 'institutional racism' is used by different people to cover a range of circumstances, and discussion of the extent of its influence and indeed even its existence is often both confused and confusing. Institutional racism describes the way in which a range of long established systems, practices and procedures, within both education and the wider society, which were originally devised to meet the needs and aspirations of a relatively homogeneous society, can now be seen not only to fail to take account of the multi-racial nature of Britain today, but may also ignore or even actively work against the interests of ethnic minority communities.

It seems to accept the concept as a description of 'the system': its outmoded procedures geared to a white society generate what Swann calls intentional and unintentional racism when these procedures are applied in a multi-ethnic society. The first is expressed in prejudices, stereotypes and racialist attacks, the second in well-meant but misguided actions that result in discrimination – for example, a teacher's emphasis on Afro-Caribbean sports expertise at the expense of aiming at academic goals in the attempt to make education more 'relevant'. Institutions, therefore, are pervaded by personal/behavioural racism: 'Institutional change and changing individual attitudes are of equal importance and have complementary roles to play in achieving the overall shift in emphasis and outlook which are essential in relation to today's multi-racial society' (*ibid*. p. 5).

In line with this, ILEA's definition (1983b, p. 16) seems to combine personal/behavioural racism and institutional racism: 'Racism may be simply identified as any attitude action or practice which assumes or implies the inherent inferiority of people with different colour, culture or ethnicity. As such it may be overt and intentional, disguised yet deliberate, or even unintentional; what has been termed "institutional racism" '. But confusingly, it goes on to define institutional racism as the prior form from which personal/behavioural racism is generated. This definition is from its acceptance of the equality perspective to underpin its anti-racism policy:

> There are certain routine practices, customs and procedures in our society whose consequence is that black people have poorer jobs, health, housing, education and life-chances than do the white majority, and less influence on the political and economic decisions which affect their lives. These practices and customs are maintained by relations and structures of power from which black people have

been and are excluded. This web of discriminatory policies, practices, and procedures is what is meant by the term 'institutional racism'

(*Ibid.* p. 21)

It is this usage that Jeffcoate criticizes for its vagueness and for its view of black people in British society as an undifferentiated lumpenproletariat. To turn to another attempt, the Berkshire policy that influenced ILEA's has a definition that again combines institutional and personal/behavioural racism:

> Racism refers to institutions and routine procedures as well as to the actions of individuals, and to unconscious and unintentional effects as well as to deliberate purposes. It summarises all attitudes, procedures and social patterns whose effect (though not necessarily whose conscious intention) is to create and maintain power, influence and well-being at the expense of Asian and Afro-Caribbean people; and whose further function is simultaneously to limit the latter to the poorest life chances and living conditions, the most menial work, and the greatest likelihood of unemployment and under-employment.

(Cited in Gaine, 1987, p. 33)

If institutional racism is 'a web of discriminatory policies, practices, and procedures', does it describe anything more than the context within which other tangible forms of racism – Jeffcoate's 'scientific' and 'popular' or Swann's intentional and unintentional – operate? There is a strong sense in which the practices of racism are supra-individual: that to define them only in personal/behavioural terms is reductionist, in the same way that claiming that all school learning can be expressed by a set of behavioural objectives reduces learning to the observable and measurable. General explanations based, for instance, on the patterns of race-awareness development in childhood might explain the similarity and incidence of personal/behavioural racism, but not why it takes the direction that it does, or why some groups in society are judged to be inferior to others as a result. To do this, arguments concerning the distribution of power and the ability of larger groups to oppress smaller groups because of their superior power have to be entered into, which brings the argument back to a consideration of structural racism. There is a distinction between the established, and changing, practices that define the way institutions operate in British society, and the racism and racialism of individuals. For example, teachers with particular views about the educability of black children may hold these as private individuals, outside the institution that defines their professional roles, but their viewpoint derives its force from their being and operating as teachers. In this more limited sense there is such a thing as institutional racism in terms of which influential role-holders hold viewpoints and operate procedures that disadvantage certain members or groups in society. But it cannot be

dismissed because it cannot be observed, or is hard to define; at the same time, the opposite viewpoint that institutions are unequivocally racist is hard to sustain. The reality is probably more piecemeal – some discriminate intentionally, others have inefficient or inconsistent procedures.

The relationship between anti-sexism as an equality initiative and different forms of sexism in society is similar to that applying to racism. Jeffcoate's four-fold racism distinction is general enough to be applicable to sexism. Thus, his 'scientific' interpretation could be applied to long-term beliefs about female capabilities, the 'popular' to prejudices and stereotypes about women's roles, while the third is translatable as sexual harassment and abuse and deliberate discrimination by individuals and groups. The same kinds of distinctions can be made between the practices and values that characterize the role of an institution in a society and the actions of those who are agents for it. The essential difference compared with race is the embeddedness of gender and its neglect as an issue in sociological research on education, for which Meighan (1986, p. 302) claims

> The reasons for this comparative neglect were complex. First, educational research followed contemporary definitions of what constituted an educational problem, and so looked at wastage of talent, inequality of opportunity, immigrant children, school-leaving ages and school organizational features. Inequality of opportunity between the sexes was rarely recognized as a problem, or at most was seen as an anachronism that would disappear with co-education. Second, sex typing appears to be a deeply embedded and taken-for-granted aspect of the social structure, so the 'common-sense' explanations about the assumed innate intellectual differences between man and woman were all too readily acceptable as a complete explanation. The lack of a well-developed comparative perspective of education may have been contributory here, since a systematic comparison with other countries (e.g. the USSR, Sweden) would have presented some disturbing information about women, education and occupations elsewhere.

Rendel's (1985) account of the debates leading up to the passing of the Sex Discrimination Act illustrates this taken-for-grantedness of gender issues and the rationalization advanced by those opposing the bill to explain and justify retaining the status quo. In analysing the motives behind the Act, she also demonstrates the higher status of race compared with gender issues at government policy-making level (Rendel, 1985, p. 93):

> Another reason for legislating was the conviction on the part of Roy Jenkins and his Special Adviser that the race relations legislation had to be strengthened. It would have been politically damaging for the Labour Party to have done nothing for women while strengthening race relations legislation. The Sex Discrimination Bill provided, as it were, a test-bed for the Race Relations Act, 1976.

The arguments advanced in support of institutional racism work in much the same way for institutional sexism but are arguably even more entrenched.

The relationship assumed between female biology – not just brain power – and natural female traits and tendencies extends to such claims that women are incapable of rational judgement when menstruating and that their emotionality compared with men makes them unfit for high managerial office. Television and newspaper advertisements can still be flagrantly and consciously sexist, but not racist. In the same way, sexual harassment can still be dismissed by its perpetrators as being non-serious, as the examples of parliamentary behaviour cited earlier here demonstrate. Ridicule and belittlement tend to characterize expressions of sexist aggression, as if women's pursuit of sex equality is taken to be unreasonable and against nature. In this, there is a measure of taken-for-granted male superiority. By contrast, racism and racialism seem motivated more by fear and the need to subjugate an alien presence: potential inferiority rather than assumed superiority? Other expressions that are more distinctive of institutional sexism, such as the continuing debate in the Anglican Church over the admitting of women priests, and the ways in which women can be prevented from getting promotion in a firm on the basis of value assumptions concerning their roles and proper responsibilities in marriage and motherhood, typify its pervasiveness and taken-for-granted qualities.

An equal-opportunities policy that is committed to combating behavioural racism and sexism in schools and that locates their causes institutionally seems, therefore, to be consistent with the nature and structure of British society.

ILEA Policy

This is certainly the case with ILEA. Its policy originated with the research commissioned by the authority into under-achievement in its primary and secondary schools. The evidence from this research was presented to school representatives in late 1981, and reviewed in the first of the six booklets comprising the equal-opportunities policy. Since several of the booklets will be referred to it will be helpful to list them*:

Race, Sex and Class. 1. Achievement in Schools (ILEA, 1983a);
Race, Sex and Class. 2. Multi-Ethnic Education in Schools (ILEA, 1983b);
Race, Sex and Class. 3. A Policy for Equality: Race (ILEA, 1983c);
Race, Sex and Class. 4. Anti-Racist Statement and Guidelines (ILEA, 1983d);
Race, Sex and Class. 5. Multi-Ethnic Education in Further, Higher and Community Education (ILEA, 1983e); and
Race, Sex and Class. 6. A Policy for Equality: Sex (ILEA, 1985a).

* Extracts reprinted with permission from ILEA Learning Resources Branch

The findings reinforce what was already known about social-class, race and gender factors affecting performance; more importantly, the first booklet moved towards policy-making by reviewing the remedies that had previously been adopted and their effectiveness, and outlining some strategies for teachers. These are the first signals of the anti-racist approach. In contrast, the advice to teachers combating gender differences is less interventionist, suggesting, for instance, monitoring single-sex teaching-group experiments and 'Implementing a school policy on equal opportunities' (ILEA, 1983a, p. 19). Its equivalent on the race list is 'Having a strong anti-racist policy on racism and providing, for older pupils, a forum for discussion of these difficult matters within the security of the school' (*ibid.*, p. 19). This emphasis on race equality is confirmed in the next four documents.

The authority, therefore, saw its main priority at the time as promoting equality for ethnic-minority groups, with class issues as a hinterland and sex equality being a prominent but less pressing undertaking, given the available resources. This can be deduced from the coverage: of the six documents incorporating the equality policy, one – the sixth, published in 1985 – concerns anti-sexism, in considerably less detail than that spent on anti-racism. An *aide-mémoire* document produced for the inspectorate in 1981 established the main line of development, of equality through anti-racist teaching, and the implementation of multi-ethnic education through replanning the curriculum in multi-ethnic terms and the maintenance of linguistic diversity. The policy formation document – 1983b – identified four inter-dependent priorities: anti-racist teaching, black representation in the authority's government, the promotion of bilingualism and the combating of black under-achievement.

Active anti-racism exercised by teachers by combating racialism and maintaining high expectations of black children are seen as the necessary conditions for successful multi-ethnic education. Reinforcing measures included more black representation in decision-making, which was implemented by establishing an Equal Opportunities Sub-Committee having an Ethnic Minorities Section, with representatives from each of the ten ILEA divisions. The right of children to be taught in their mother tongue was taken to be a corner-stone for multi-ethnicity in the curriculum; all children should understand something of the languages spoken by their minority-group peers. But under-achievement is seen as the crucial factor. The inflexibility of the examination system is attacked, and the rise of supplementary schools as a result of black families' lack of confidence in the mainstream schools is regarded as a challenge. Under-achievement measured by a lack of examination success is for the schools to remedy.

This stance is re-asserted by the analysis of assimilation, integration, cultural pluralism and equality – in 1983b – as available perspectives, and the choice of the equality perspective to underpin anti-racism. The main criterion for assessing the first two is the racism index – assimilation is condemned out of hand for being racist:

> What is wrong with this perspective is that:
>
> (i) It defines the black communities as 'the problem', and therefore not only fails to challenge negative views about black people but also actually promotes and strengthens such views, both in the education service and in society.
> (ii) It is racist because it is based on, and communicates, a notion of white cultural superiority. This is damaging to white people as well as black.
>
> *(Ibid.* p. 20)

Cultural diversity receives limited approval but is rejected because of its inadequate treatment of racism:

> This perspective represents a decisive departure from the explicit racism of the first approach. Nevertheless:
>
> (ii) It conceives of racism as merely a set of mental prejudices held by a smallish number of unenlightened white people, and hence ignores or denies the structural aspects of racism, both in the education system and in society. . . .
> (iv) It ignores the issue which black people themselves consider to be of vital importance – that is, the issue of racism and the promotion of racial equality.
>
> *(Ibid.)*

In discussing the equality perspective, the document begins with the unequivocal, 'This perspective will inform all the work of the Authority' *(ibid.* p. 21). Appendix B is a further explication of anti-racism and provides the reference-points for schools' and colleges' anti-racist policies; while each institution has some room for manoeuvre in devising a policy to fit its particular circumstances, the document details a number of elements that are required of all:

> There will be:
>
> 3. A clear indication of what is not acceptable and the procedures, including sanctions, to deal with any transgressions.
> 4. An explanation of the way in which the school or college intends to develop practices which both tackle racism and create educational opportunities which make for a cohesive society and a local school or college community in which diversity can flourish.
>
> *(Ibid.* p. 25)

Teachers studying this document will be very clear as to their required behaviour as role models, but it is not until the second-to-last page that the document begins to consider what they might teach, in the name of anti-racism. The discussion is more about the organizational contexts of teaching and learning with some reference to the school's climate and ethos, with just one section on curriculum content and resources. Since there are no further guidelines offered for curricular development, it seems to be assumed that multi-ethnic education will emerge, once teachers have assimilated the equality perspective and its anti-racist implications. Here, some cross-references to the curricular guidelines that ILEA, along with other local authorities, has been producing in response to the DES Circular 14/77 review would have given the policy-making a more practical edge. As Bash *et al.* (1985) point out, the policy seems to be abandoning ground won by the authority's earlier multi-ethnic innovations.

By contrast, both with the race documents and with the pioneering work carried out by the equal-opportunities inspectorate, the sixth document on sex equality is almost perfunctory. It signals the higher priority of race compared with gender issues. The statement itself reiterates in general terms the causes and effects of sexism and recognizes the potential for education to both transmit and challenge values. The supporting argument takes much the same general line in discussing sex-stereotyping, achievement and the effects of the hidden curriculum. The detail of what constitutes anti-sexist behaviour, how and why teachers should combat it and how schools should go about formulating an anti-sexist policy is in an accompanying booklet (1985b). Perhaps the strongest aspect of the supporting argument is the alignment of sexism and racism as being 'linked through the experience of discrimination, prejudice, stereotyping and powerlessness' (ILEA, 1985a, p. 5).

This alignment is developed in the implementation document of the anti-sexism part of the equality policy, *Implementing the ILEA's Anti-Sexist Policy* (ILEA, 1985b). It differs from the anti-racist programme both in presentation and approach, being virtually a blueprint for school-based policy formation that gives schools considerable freedom of manoeuvre compared with the top-down style of the anti-racist policy. Its three sections, identifying sexism, bringing about change and planning a programme for action, delineate a process beginning with sensitizing staff to sexist practices leading to classroom-based and school programmes. What emerges from this is a specification for anti-sexist teaching and learning that is considerably more detailed than that for anti-racism. The format is very much like that for the earlier, race, *aide-mémoire* (ILEA, 1981), which continues to be the authority's most-developed general statement on the nature of multi-ethnic education, though later booklets such as *Education in a Multiethnic Society. The Primary School* (ILEA, 1984) develop some of the lines of action laid down in the policy documents. The anti-sexism implementation booklet in fact draws upon the *aide-mémoire* by linking anti-sexism and anti-racism strategies:

> Many schools have gone through the process of developing an anti-racist policy before looking at anti-sexism. Some schools have considered the two issues closely together, some separately. Anti-sexist practice must also be anti-racist, and while a separate focus may be helpful, schools will want to bring together the two initiatives in practice.

What can be learnt from the experience of developing an anti-racist policy that can help in dealing with anti-sexism?
Can the same structures and procedures be used?
How can experience of curricular innovation be used?
How can the curriculum and materials be monitored for all forms of prejudice and stereotyping?

(ILEA, 1985b, p. 11)

ILEA Policy: Implementation

The implementation of the anti-racist policy is marked by urgency and compulsion:

> It follows that every aspect of the Authority's work, every branch and every institution must be examined with the clear objective of eradicating racist practices and assumptions. The responsibility for developing and implementing the Authority's anti-racist policies must rest with every employee in every institution and every branch of the Authority's administration. It is for every institution and branch of the Authority therefore, to develop a coherent action programme for the elimination of racist practices.

(ILEA, 1983d, p. 3)

and:

> Each school and college will finally determine its policy in the light of its own circumstances. However, certain elements are common to all. There will be:
>
> 1. A clear, unambiguous statement of opposition to any form of racism or racist behaviour.
> 2. A firm expression of all pupils' or students' rights to the best possible education.
> 3. A clear indication of what is not acceptable and the procedures, including sanctions, to deal with any transgressions.
> 4. An explanation of the way in which the school or college intends to develop practices which both tackle racism and create educational opportunities which make for a cohesive society and a local school or college community in which diversity can flourish.
> 5. An outline of the measures by which development will be monitored and evaluated.

(*Ibid.* p. 5)

This closely-directed, top-down strategy for anti-racism contrasts with the school- and classroom-based approach adopted for implementing anti-sexist education:

> There is no blueprint for exactly how to proceed. Rather, it is suggested that each school considers what is most appropriate for its particular stage of development. Attitudes, awareness, concerns and priorities vary between schools and change over time.
>
> While discussion and commitment to a policy is important, it is only part of the longer, slower process of bringing about educational change.] Transforming policy into practice is essential if girls and boys are to receive an education which is genuinely anti-sexist and anti-racist. This is an education which enables them to achieve their full potential, unrestricted because of their sex, or their race or class.
>
> (ILEA, 1985b, Introduction)

While both the race and the sex policy define the perspective for schools, the second virtually makes schools autonomous in the ways they might formulate their programmes. There is no immediate explanation as to why the anti-sexism approach, in which internal dialogue and negotiation leading to individual processes of implementation and development, is substituted for a vigorous, action-plan-based, top-down strategy. A practical reason for this more school-based approach may lie in the considerable earlier expense of effort on the part of teachers implementing anti-racism strategies, combined with the on-going task of producing whole-school curricular guidelines – also at a time of falling roles in primary schools, teacher redeployment and cuts, as the case-study of policy formation at Ennersdale School in Chapter 7 makes clear. The effects of long-term industrial action by teachers meant that, up to the imposition of the 1987 pay award (with its directed time 'Baker hours' accompaniment), staff meetings outside school time were proscribed in many schools that limited the amount of time available for planning whole-school policies and programmes. A further question concerns the relative effectiveness of top-down compared with school-based approaches, when teachers have to assimilate policies that some find to be extreme. It is possible, considering all these factors, that had the authority adopted the same top-down style for anti-sexism, it would have met with opposition and antagonism from schools already overloaded by a plethora of outside-dictated innovation. Anecdotal evidence suggests that in an eighteen-months period in the mid-1980s, an Inner London primary school would have received about thirty documents from local and central sources, all requiring responses. A combination of overload and low morale could have resulted in opposition or token action.

A Comparison: Kent County Council Education Authority –
Equal Opportunities in the Curriculum

This is one of the most recent policies, having been published in February 1988. It is markedly different in several ways from ILEA's policy in its central concern with gender inequality, in its status as an advisory, guidelines' document for schools to follow and in its explication of inequality as discriminatory behaviour rather than being institutional. Its orientation is at the sex-equitable/egalitarian point on the continuum table (Table 3.1) in Chapter 3. Its concern with gender inequalities might be seen as characteristic of non-inner-city education authorities with a high proportion of all-white schools (though there is a concentration of mainly Asian groups in parts of north Kent). Swann's 'education for all' seems to have had little impact on the policy Working Party.

The policy statement makes a distinction between overt and covert sex discrimination; overt sexism that is illegal under the Sex Discrimination Act occurs, for example, in option choices, examination entry and careers guidance. Covert discrimination

> is much more difficult to identify and to address. It relates to the assumptions, beliefs and values, acquired over a long period of time, which affect people's instinctive responses. . . . The Authority recognises that progress in eliminating this kind of discrimination will best be achieved by education and persuasion rather than by instruction and imperatives.
>
> (Kent County Council Education, 1988, p. 3)

The last sentence signals the nature of the authority's implementation procedure. While it regards discrimination as unacceptable, it aims to eliminate it by changing staff attitudes through disseminating literature, guidelines for good practice and providing in-service courses rather than imposing viewpoints and practices from the centre. In Chin's (1968) terms, a normative re-educative rather than a power-coercive strategy will be used. The authority limits itself to such centrally-initiated moves as changing the designations of head master/mistress to head teacher, and senior master/ mistress to deputy head, and to recommending that most of one of the five INSET 'Baker days' in 1988–9 be used by schools to discuss equal opportunities. More generally, it recommends that the job descriptions for the inspectorate should include the promotion of equal opportunities in the curriculum and in induction, and that in-service programmes should also promote this.

This permeation-of-attitudes approach extends to the recommendations to schools. These include the possibility of making a staff member responsible for promoting and monitoring equal opportunities, including an equality statement in the curriculum policy and reviewing teaching materials. The recommendations are moderate to the point of innocuousness, but the advice to school-governing bodies is even more so: 'That in relation to their responsibilities under Section 18 of the Education Act 1986, Governing Bodies be encouraged to assume some responsibility for ensuring that there is equality of opportunity in their schools' (*ibid.* p. 4). The final three pages of the eight-page document present some figures from recently-conducted surveys. They include examination results and YTS placements that reinforce previous evidence for gender inequality in outcomes in schools. The last page gives some data from a questionnaire survey of 180 Kent schools conducted in the summer term 1987. Without the lead given by a local-authority policy, very few schools had their own or had designated teachers having responsibility for equal opportunities, but a quarter of primary and half the secondary schools felt that the authority should be giving a lead in promoting equality, especially through in-service training. There is more than a suggestion here that the schools would have accepted a harder-line implementation approach than the one adopted, which seems to have been tailored to the attitudes and perceptions of Kent school governors rather than the teachers. This might be tactically sound, considering the increased powers given to governing bodies under the 1988 Act, but it might not win the support of those Kent teachers who regard equal opportunities as a central issue. Also, why the concentration on gender equality under the umbrella of equal opportunities for all? The distancing effect of having a majority of schools that are all white might account for this, setting aside such questions discussed earlier here as to whom multicultural education is for. Also, gender inequalities can be seen to be less contentious and problematic than inequalities concerning race. Given the embeddedness of gender inequality, the availability of evidence concerning access and out-come can be doubled-edged in its effects: it can demonstrate the fact of boy–girl inequalities in schools or it can be used to sustain the stereotypes projected by peoples' beliefs in sex-based, naturally-different abilities and interests. Inequality issues concerning gender are simply less threatening, more easily dismissed and more susceptible to token responses from official bodies than ones concerning race. Since 1981 especially, race has generated foreboding because of its volatility, and the threats that race issues offer to white society's sense of well-being ensures that there will continue to be government responses in the form of commissions and policies. So far, there have been no sex riots.

The Foreword of the Kent policy draws attention to the wastage of talent arising from gender inequalities, a legimate standpoint concerning access and performance. It also emphasizes the authority–school partnership strategy in policy implementation. But the material from the authority's own survey suggests that many schools would like to see it leading the implementation rather than recommending how schools should proceed virtually independently.

Implementation Strategies

The ILEA and Kent approaches are contrasted and there are questions as to the effectiveness of one strategy compared with another. The *laissez-faire*, Schools Council project implementation type of approach with its consequences of uneven take-up contrasts with the no-negotiation conditions of top-down innovation that do not necessarily percolate down into every classroom. What is involved in these are two conflicting interpretations of the teacher's role in innovation, and of teacher professionality, in which ILEA's sex and race policies are vividly contrasted. On the one hand, an anti-racist and anti-sexist stance has been adopted by the authority as serving the best interests of Inner London children, with the expectation that since teachers are the prime agents of their children's educational interests they will accept the wisdom of this approach and will collaborate in implementing it. The local-authority–school partnership is stressed; depending on the amount of autonomy it gives to schools to interpret and implement the central policy according to what they understand to be their own conditions and their children's educational needs, it can be seen as an enhancement of professionality, beyond immediate classroom concerns. It typifies Hoyle's (1975) extended, as opposed to restricted, teacher professionality.

On the other hand, imposed from the centre innovation, which is tightly monitored, has the effect of reducing teachers' professionality by denying them the autonomy to make their own curricular or organizational decisions, except of a technical kind. The exercise of autonomy at classroom level continues to be important to teachers' professional identity, especially in primary schools. A strong top-down policy can have the effect of defining for teachers what their children's needs should be. Teachers who are convinced cultural pluralists rather than anti-racists, for example, could claim with some justice that they are being prevented from acting in the best interests of their children. At the county-hall level, the anti-racist policy especially is a classic attempt at social engineering – ambitious, doctrinaire and radical. At the school level, it is as if the authority has decided that such social engineering is too important to leave to teachers.

Given some of the research evidence for teachers' resistance to change (for example, Stenhouse, 1975; Easen, 1985), the authority may be right. At

the same time, in contradiction to its intentions, the policy and its implementation style have given teachers considerable room for manoeuvre in
responding. Teachers need good reasons before they commit themselves
wholeheartedly to the dangerous business of change; top-down strategies
are apparently cohesive but can actually divide a staff. To teachers who
agree with the official line, there will be every reason to implement it. Many
teachers in ILEA would assert that the equality policy has made them better
teachers. For those with political and professional objections to it, there is
scope for avoiding action, particularly if they see no room for debate. Their
reasoning is on the lines that since the policy was imposed on them and they
could claim they were not consulted as professionals, their allegiance cannot
legitimately be claimed, except for their contractual obligations as
employees.

So the opposite argument can be applied: equal-opportunities policies are
too important to be the subject of rigorous top-down innovation. The
avoidance of token change, of Hoyle's condition of innovation without
change, depends on teachers' not only recognizing the validity of the
potential innovation but also exercising ownership over it. The degree of
professional awareness needed to achieve this depends on teachers having
the autonomy to debate and to resolve issues and to develop policies in their
own schools. What is crucial to this is the way power in the system is located
and legitimized – how much schools should have compared with local
authorities. ILEA's position is summed up well by the Ennersdale staff in
the case-study in Chapter 7; their judgement was that the authority had defined the problem which was seen as a legitimate act, but it had also gone on
to define the solution. Ennersdale and other schools like it had a long history
of developing multicultural principles and practices. Were these being
ignored or set aside to make way for a new definitive view held by
county-hall politicians?

Looking at the situation from the point of view of practice, it is also true
that teachers have to be sure of their competency before risking change in
their schools and classrooms. Change strongly depends upon a positive
climate, which is generated in a school by such factors as consultative
leadership; recognition of professional expertise and interests by head
teachers and between peers; efficient and appropriate resourcing (including
adequate time to evaluate proposals); and hidden-curricular factors such as
high morale, group cohesion and sufficient institutional confidence to be
able to call in experts as consultants. Miles's (1975) concept of a school's
'organizational health' summarizes some of the conditions needed for
successful institutional change. Stenhouse (1975), through his experience of
the Humanities Curriculum Project, made a convincing analysis of factors

that undermine potential change and that focus on a school's equilibrium. In particular, he draws on the notion of temporary professional incompetence that affects teachers during the early stages of innovation.

McDonald and Walker's (1976) notion of curricular negotiation is relevant to the debate on how the responsibility for equal-opportunities implementation might be distributed between schools and local authorities in that it recognizes the power factor in innovation and is the antithesis of top-down. It derives from their experience of large-scale, centre-periphery, Schools Council project dissemination. What is implemented is what is negotiated between developers and teachers – centre and periphery in fact change places: 'In terms of permanence and power it is the schools and the L.E.A.s that constitute the centre; projects and even the Council itself, are marginal, precarious, temporary. . . . The developers command no one and can afford to offend very few (*ibid.* pp. 47–8). This is the antithesis to the monitored, holistic approach reinforced by the power a local authority has over its schools through its politicians, officers and resources agencies. At the same time, negotiation between schools and the authority in some form and to some degree will be essential to a considered as distinct from a token response to the requirement to innovate.

The argument, therefore, is that innovation, especially that concerning equality policies, requires a partnership in which, broadly, the power to initiate is with the local authority and the power to implement is with the schools. This entails that innovation is essentially but not exclusively school based. The claim is not new: Skilbeck made it several years ago in his criticisms of systems theories applied to change (1971), and Stenhouse's (1975) conception of the teacher as curriculum researcher upheld it. This viewpoint is operable in quasi-decentralized education systems of the kind that still exist in Britain, in spite of over a decade of growing central direction that culminated in the Education Act 1988. But it stops short of claiming that teachers should be the sole arbiters of change. At least one piece of research evidence (Wicksteed and Hill, 1979) suggests that primary teachers understand the shared nature of this responsibility. *Laissez-faire*, classroom-based innovation is potentially anti-policy since it asserts the dominance of the individual over the institution. But school-based innovation entailing collective decision-making in which a measure of classroom autonomy is retained suggests the means by which local-authority policies can be implemented on the school's terms without distortion or compromise:

> Thus school-based curriculum development is predicated upon the concept, admittedly idealised, of teachers who creatively reconstruct the curriculum within a recognised framework of local and national expectations; it is not predicated upon passive acceptance of external definitions of the curriculum, or the myth of

the 'autonomous' school, existing independently of its political and economic context.

(*Ibid.* p. 34)

What seems to be in doubt, however, is the continuing ability of schools to respond creatively to the requirement to innovate in a system in which there is growing central control: quasi-centralization rather than decentralization. In an education system, school autonomy is diminished by the extent to which central government makes decisions that are binding and not merely advisory on local government and, therefore, on schools – in such crucial areas as curriculum content, the monitoring of pupil attainment and teachers' conditions of service including appraisal.

The key indicators since 1976 are not encouraging. They include DES Circular 14/77 requiring local authorities to produce curricular guidelines for school use, a form of central control that exploits the DES–local authority partnership; the abolition of the teacher and local-authority controlled Schools Council in 1984; the rise of the Assessment of Performance Unit, initially as a monitoring body but increasingly perceived as a means by which national norms of achievement can be developed and operated; and the range of DES and HMI policy formation and discussion papers published since 1977 defining and redefining the curriculum from 5 to 16. More recently there have been the criteria for teacher-education courses imposed on institutions by the DES through its quango, the Committee for the Accreditation of Teacher Education (CATE), which, for instance, imposes subject study at honours level for two out of the four years of a primary batchelor-of-education honours-degree course, thereby creating a centrally-defined batchelor of education in the face of CNAA and university validation, and redefining the nature and role of primary teachers in subject-specialist terms. And, of course, most recently, the package of legislation included in the 1988 Act, imposing a subject-based, centrally-directed curriculum for State schools, with bench-mark testing, strong advice on how much time should be spent on core and foundation subjects, opting out clauses for schools and the abolition of ILEA. These provisions raise more general questions about the possibilities of implementing equal opportunities, discussed in Chapter 8.

Many teachers will want to assert that much of this legislation means central control in general terms only; that little of it, including the curricular measures, will percolate down to primary schools in particular during the life of the present government. But this overlooks certain historical factors. Lawton's (1980) 'Golden Age of Teacher Freedom', from which the common-sense belief in teachers' classroom autonomy in Britain originated, was a relatively short period, from post-1945 to the mid-1970s; it had everything to do with local authorities' autonomy, defined by the Education Act 1944, being delegated as professional autonomy to the schools. With the emphasis now on more direct forms of accountability, schools to local authorities, and local authorities to the DES, teacher autonomy is likely to be reduced as a consequence as teachers increasingly come under public scrutiny by parents, governing bodies, employers and the DES through the new conditions of service. The cumulative effect of centralism and direct accountability could create a climate in which school-based innovation is hazardous in problematic areas such as anti-racism, but perhaps not sex-equitable schooling.

But this would only be brought about by a full-blooded, centrally-directed system such as the French or the Swedish, in which not only the curriculum but also subject-time allocation, textbooks and learning resources are generally prescribed by the State. What is intended by the Act – though this has been hard to judge as clauses are added to it in its passage through Parliament – appears to retain enough of the decentralized system to allow local authorities space to interpret in their responses to central-government policy. Since local authorities are likely to continue to delegate responsibilities for internal organization and curriculum development, schools should retain a measure of their professional independence. A fully-centralized system would indeed be radical, and would need a new and initially-expensive infrastructure to make it workable, and governable.

With the increase in central control and the development of local-authority curricular guidelines and whole-school policy-making, the age of *laissez-faire* 'hero-innovator' change was already passing. Miles's (1964) argument that the staff group rather than the individual teacher in his or her classroom is the innovatory unit is appropriate to equality policy-making because of the way it requires the staff as a whole to agree on a policy. ILEA's school-based, anti-sexism guidelines are very much an exemplar for this approach.

5
EQUALITY POLICY-MAKING:
THE SCHOOL AND THE TEACHERS

While schools exercise limited power over the external conditions in which they operate, they have considerably more in developing the internal organization and procedures necessary for innovation. In equality policy-formation, greater staff cohesion in the decision and policy-making process can be brought about by a collegial structure in a school, in which individual responsibilities are clearly identified and shared. The strategies of policy-making will depend for their success on the staff working to agreed goals.

The School: Ethos and Autonomy

Stenhouse (1975) made the point in the mid-1970s that it is pertinent to ask how far schools are free to change, considering the constraints acting upon them from the outside world. He was writing at a time of educational cuts and not surprisingly he took the major constraint to be lack of resources followed by parental and social opinion. These conditions still apply at the end of the 1980s but are overshadowed by the DES centralization initiatives discussed in the last chapter. His question refers to the amount of independence schools might have within the web of social, economic and political contexts – local and national – that control them and define their purposes. Inevitably, these also influence the ways teachers perceive their roles, as keepers of the status quo or as innovators. As Dalton (1988) demonstrates, schools and teachers, particularly if they are undergoing change whether internally or externally generated, are subject to number of reality definers –

local authority and DES policy, parents' expectations, pupil-control factors – that limit and direct innovation. It is the combination of these constantly-changing and sometimes unpredictable factors that generate a school's particular identity or ethos; in doing this they also define the extent of its potential autonomy. By this is meant the potential its staff has to change its internal organization, patterns of learning and teaching and the attitudes and perceptions of teachers and pupils. This is paradoxical, since a school does not discover how much autonomy it has until or unless it embarks on change. A school that has high status in its neighbourhood among parents, pupils and its local authority is likely to have the institutional self-confidence to initiate reforms with the expectation that they will be accepted by parents and others after the inevitable period of uncertainty. Such a school would also expect to be able to attract the local authority's attention in the need for new resources or outside expertise.

There are direct connections between the nature of a school's ethos, amount of autonomy – the potential to innovate – a school has, and the level of its morale. A major barrier to innovation is low morale, and at a time of severe financial restraints, rising class sizes, negative media treatment of State education and increasing central direction, morale is bound to be a major problem in schools. At a time when *ad hoc* innovation undertaken by individual teachers in their own classrooms is giving way to staff – group-based, whole-school policy-making with a strong element of compulsion from outside behind it, the conditions for innovation have probably never been more difficult.

Stenhouse, considering secondary schools, claimed that control was the most important barrier to change, because of the conscript nature of school populations; control depends on equilibrium being maintained, which is antithetical to innovation. There are, of course, problems of control in primary schools; they tend to be less predictable, more face to face and less orchestrated by groups because of the nature of the primary age-range, but they have the same inhibiting effect on innovation. Part of the problem of control is caused by the temporary deskilling of teachers brought about by the need to discard old methods and acquire the skills to operate new ones in implementing change, and this applies to all types of learning institutions. MacDonald (1975, p. 170), in evaluating Stenhouse's Humanities Curriculum Project in schools, noted how a teacher could appear to be temporarily incompetent to pupils when he or she was acquiring new skills:

> Incompetent pupils, incompetent teachers. Incompetent Project? Not necessarily. Genuine innovation begets incompetence. It deskills teacher and pupil alike, suppressing acquired competences and demanding the development of new ones. . . . In the end the discomfort will be resolved one way or the other, by

reversion to previous practice or by achieving new skills, and new frameworks. But the discomfort and dismay are built in; they are defining characteristics of innovation.

Low morale will ensure that the threat of classroom disorder will be avoided by perfunctory compliance with the innovation proposals. Thus, morale and control are strongly related.

Another set of potential barriers concern the school's image to the world outside. These can be summed up as its moral identity, as Stenhouse (1975, p. 169) puts it: 'The school exercises great power over its pupil population and through these hostages power over parents. There is thus an acute need to justify the way that power is used. As a consequence, schools often assume a position of rectitude'. This power has both its actual and its symbolic faces: in primary schools, parents do hand their children over to teachers to be 'schooled'. Schools often have recourse to ideologies that refer to general educational benefits rather than individual performance when they seek to justify changes to parents and others outside. When a school is considering changes to a key, basic-skills area such as language – for example, moving from a graded reading-scheme approach to using collections of books in teaching reading – the justifications are likely to centre on how this change will generate interest and motivate children to want to read. The reasons will be couched ideologically, in terms of educational growth, as much as or rather than instrumentally in terms of performance. But parents, unless they are particularly knowledgeable, will not always connect the two. Their concern for the performance of their own children – exacerbated by their smaller amount of power in the situation – usually means that more general considerations of what might be of educational benefit to the children as a whole are over-ridden. This location-of-power dimension lies behind the child-centred stance of many schools. Arguably, it enables them to be child-centred, but it can cause tensions. For example, parents' concern with their children's academic achievements can place a strain on the teacher–parent collaboration ideology of many infant schools.

All of these connected factors apply in the case of equal-opportunities innovation. There is also the need to identify, debate and reconcile teachers' personal values and beliefs as these impinge on policy formation. So-called 'routine' innovation concerning curricular and organizational change first requires that teachers assimilate the proposals within their personal ideologies of teaching and learning and, second, calls upon their technical skills and expertise. But devising, for example, an anti-sexism statement and implementing its curricular, organizational and resourcing implications may, as a precondition, require teachers to re-assess their more wide-ranging personal viewpoints – for example, about ascribed gender roles in society, the class structure and the exercise of power. If the new questions and issues can be tested in the classroom, perhaps by teachers considering the amount of attention they pay to boys compared with girls, or the extent to which the learning activities they provide are influenced by the range of known and potential interests among their children, then their application and effects will be harder to reject as irrelevant 'theory'.

In order to do this, teachers and schools need to create ideological and practical room for themselves. In view of the discussion about school and local-authority responsibilities in the previous chapter, schools will need the independence to be able to appraise the local-authority viewpoint in terms of their own analysis of children's needs. This is not achieved easily: it is necessary for a school to develop and sustain an identity through how its staff prefer to operate by being highly valued in a neighbourhood by parents, children and the local authority. This, of course, does not necessarily mean that it has to be child-centred; another kind of ideological position and way of operating that can meet with parental approval entails children wearing uniforms, having good manners and being deferential to adults, but also being competitive and achieving highly in basic-skills learning. But it is hard to see how any other than a socially-oriented child-centred regime could be a suitable context for promoting equality. This in itself might be a develop-ment point for some schools.

This is not a plea for school autonomy in the sense that the school alone should be responsible for innovation; Campbell's (1985) points cited here earlier, that school-based innovation needs to work within a reference frame comprising local and national expectations, acknowledges other legitimate interests. In any case, it is difficult now for a school staff to ignore those expectations that take the form of DES or local-authority curriculum directives, while changes such as those to governing-body membership and the requirement to produce school brochures mean that the local com-munity is now more involved in a school's internal organization. Skilbeck (1984) also makes the point about interdependence and the distribution of authority this entails in his discussion of the OECD/CERI project on school-based curriculum development. An overarching conclusion from this long-term study is that the school's demands for more independence in curriculum development are legitimized as being part of a broader move-ment in Western societies for more participation in decision-making. In education systems this has arisen because of the rigidity of top-down approaches and the under-resourcing or poor design of centre-periphery initiatives of the Schools-Council type in innovation. Schools as complex, organic, social institutions need a measure of self-direction and determina-tion if they are to thrive, and are best placed to identify their pupils' learning needs and to service these. This task requires schools to adapt curricular frameworks that accord with local needs; moreover, he argues, 'Teacher self-actualisation, motivation and sense of achievement are integrally bound up with curriculum decision making which is the staple of teachers' professional lives' (*ibid.* p.15).

Against this case there are doubts about the competence of teachers as a body to maintain development, or whether they are predisposed to change; also, there are questions as to whether schools can be organized for sustained change, and whether this is the most cost-effective way to innovate. More oblique problems are those of localism, parochialism and conservatism:

> Much that goes on under the name of school-based curriculum development, while it may well be a kind of highly practical and adaptive small-scale innovation in a particular part of the curriculum, lacks any significance for the overall curriculum of a school or a system of education. Sometimes, school-based curriculum development may simply mask a conservative resistance to a much needed general review, or serve as a diversionary measure to avoid challenge on more basic issues.
>
> (*Ibid.* pp. 17–18)

In conclusion, he suggests 'By building in school-based curriculum development as a crucial component of a systemwide style of curriculum review, evaluation and development, we may find that the school's role in the curriculum becomes clearer and more manageable than it has appeared to many of its critics in recent years' (*ibid.* p. 18).

Collegiality

At face value, curriculum development and the notion of collegiality applied to schools go together. Collegiality refers to the original idea of a college; it entails teachers having collective responsibility for all decisions that affect teaching and learning. Each would have equal status but would contribute different curricular expertise; Campbell (1985) suggests that it emphasizes relationships between colleagues expressed in terms of collaboration in decision-making through the pooling of subject expertise. This notion of a community of professionals has great attractions from the point of view of developing extended as distinct from restricted professionality as the necessary basis for innovation. Yet Hoyle (1986) asserts that schools, because of their inherent divisiveness and hierarchical organization, are not collegial by nature. Again, his claim applies more to the complexities, size and administrative strata characteristic of secondary schools rather than the more face-to-face, informal situation of primaries. Campbell presents a balanced, if cautious argument for the development of collegiality in primary schools, reinforced by the case-studies of innovation and recent research he documents on staff relationships. But he acknowledges its potential. Hoyle (1986, p. 87) offers criteria that would characterize a collegial school:

1. Teachers would integrate their work on a team basis.
2. The teams would have internal democracy and leadership would be variable or rotating.
3. The teams would determine their own objectives in the light of school goals.
4. School goals would be determined by a collegium in which all professional members of staff would participate.
5. The chairmanship of the collegium would be the chief executive role.
6. The collegium would have an administrative staff.
7. Evaluation of teacher performance would be by fellow professionals.

He suggests several difficulties in implementing these conditions. A major problem is the legal authority of the head teacher and the clear lines of accountability between heads and local authorities. This would seem to entail that the head be the permanent chair as chief executive but having to live with the possibility of being voted down. He also argues that teachers' salary scales incorporating a number of status levels is an obstacle, but now, as a result of the 1987 pay and conditions award and the creation of a main scale, some of this divisiveness has gone. However, this has created another dilemma. Under the old scale-post system, teachers had clearly-designated and rewarded curricular and organizational responsibilities and could be expected by their heads to lead innovation according to their own expertise. Now, with the creation of curriculum co-ordinators on a temporary incentive-payment basis, with the head in a more powerful position than before to sponsor particular areas of development in the school, responsibilities are more onerous and less secure. So, equality of status via salary is achieved through the main scale but the exercise of individual expertise becomes more a matter of volunteering and internal bargaining than formal acknowledgement via salary. So innovation will be influenced even more by collective intrinsic and perhaps altruistic motivation than previously, when there was also a recognizable measure of extrinsic motivation through the awarding of Scale 2 and 3 posts.

Hoyle claims that collegial schools could become as bureaucratic as organizations that are consciously bureaucratic, resulting in teachers having less freedom of action in their own classrooms. He argues that this can happen at the levels of policy-making, planning and pedagogy: at each level group decisions are made, which of their nature reduce individual teacher autonomy. As he comments, 'There is a cost to collegiality which is the loss of some freedom of action. It would remain to be seen whether this loss was outweighed by consequent gains in the collective control of the professional activities of a group of colleagues' (*ibid*. p. 89). But this collective control is more likely to safeguard autonomy than having a whole-school policy formulated by a single person in authority, such as the head or deputy. What is under scrutiny here is the amount of individual autonomy possible or allowable in operating a whole-school policy. This develops the point made earlier, that when teachers are involved in whole-school policy-making, they gain in professional responsibility at the cost of relinquishing some of their classroom freedom. Because of the face-to-face situation of most primary schools with their small staffs and simple hierarchical arrangements, this trade-off may be more pronounced than in the larger and more bureaucratically-organized secondary schools, where authority figures can be more easily evaded in the interests of pursuing one's own course. In larger primary schools, it will be necessary to create small working groups to develop parts of the policy, and these tend to take on a life of their own. The time they extract from teachers' 'free' time can be resented. From the viewpoint of structure, there is the question of how much decision-making authority a working party should have. If this is not settled its actions can raise the emotional temperature in a school to the extent that its work becomes counter-productive because it is distrusted by outsiders. Does it only make recommendations to the head? Or the whole staff? Or does it come up with policy decisions that are confirmed by the head, or the staff? Is it able to call upon outside experts such as advisory teachers or inspectors independently of the head? Should it have some claim on resources including school finances? Although a group's terms of reference can be specifically defined, it can be more difficult to designate the areas and limits of its responsibility in practice. Too specific a designation can result in frustrating the group's aims, while if it is too general, the group can become too free-floating. As Hoyle says (*ibid*. p. 90),

> In bureaucratic and structurally loose systems there is no doubt where the power (i.e. authority) lies. It lies with the head and is delegated through the hierarchy. In a collegial system authority is diffuse. It appears not to lie with committees but somehow *between* committees. . . . Thus, in a collegial system there is the frustration of not knowing where power lies and *in having nobody to blame*.

Finally, although collegiality is conceptually opposed to bureaucracy because of its emphasis on professional collaboration, the aims of a collegial school are likely to be pursued through bureaucratic devices such as committees and working parties. The problem is that these can actually obstruct rather than foster change, in the manner of normal bureaucracies.

What might collegiality offer to primary schools, particularly those developing equality policies? Its problems of bureaucratic organization and procedure, to which Hoyle draws attention, apply arguably to larger organizations than the typical primary school, but it still offers challenges as a mode of policy-making and innovation that is unfamiliar to many teachers. Campbell's (1985) is probably the most developed viewpoint, arising from his case-studies of school-based development. He argues that collegiality is the current model of good primary practice as disseminated by the HMI since their junior school survey, *Primary Education in England* (DES, 1978). His account of collegiality very much accords with Hoyle's in its defining characteristics. These include small working parties of teachers making recommendations for innovation to the staff as a whole, who then make decisions. The groups are led by curriculum post-holders who draw upon expertise inside and outside the school. Their change-agent role is central, since they contribute not only from their curricular expertise but also through their ability to maintain the social climate needed to ensure development. The image is that of self-evaluating teachers with a high commitment to professional development. The head's role is essentially that of co-ordinator, resource manager and first among equals in delegating specific responsibilities to working groups.

A distinctive ethos is created in which role expectations are clearly communicated and understood and where there is collective accountability for defining and meeting learning needs. Such an ethos results in considerable job satisfaction.

Campbell (1985, p. 153) points out that unlike previous models of primary-school practice, this one emphasizes teachers: 'In the foreground of this image is not the school's organisation, or children's emotional adjustment, or community relationships, but working groups of teachers engaged in the process of developing school-wide policies and practices for the curriculum'. The notion that successful innovation depends upon teacher development is not new, though it encompasses several viewpoints that can be summed up as the individual versus the group. Miles, working in the USA in 1960s, suggested a number of criteria under the heading 'organizational health', mentioned in the previous chapter, which can be applied to a school to determine whether or not its climate is conducive to change. His work on what he describes as temporary systems (Miles, 1964) emphasizes the group rather than individual teachers as the innovatory unit. Hoyle broadly accepted the notion of organizational health in considering what he describes as 'tissue rejection', when a proposed innovation does not 'take' because the school's social system rejects it. Stenhouse's (1975) concept of the teacher as curriculum researcher is a powerful argument for teacher development, though it extolls the individual teacher-innovator rather than

Miles's group. Another parallel line of development considers the head-teacher's role as leader of innovation. Stenhouse reviewed four decision-making styles that range from authoritarian to democratic, and suggests that consultation, by which heads make decisions based on dialogue with their staff is the emergent one. This asserts the necessity for heads to make the final decisions because of their legal responsibilities to governing bodies and local authorities. But Campbell sees head teachers in a supporting rather than a leading role and identifies a number of strategies they used in his case-study schools to maintain school-based innovation. These hardly ever involved traditional leadership, but emphasized resource provision and management, delegating responsibilities and defining roles and responsibilities. His heads are managers rather than leaders of innovation.

This conception of headship accords with collegiality since central to the notion is the recognition of individual expertise and experience and the authority delegated to exercise these. Because of the complex social, professional and personal interactions and relationships involved, what, of course, is also crucial is the right kind of head in terms of personal qualities. Campbell's description of heads (1985, p. 109) as vicarious curriculum developers summarizes this complexity and subtlety of judgement required:

> They recognise initiative, encourage postholders, provide useful back-up support of a practical kind and in a number of ways confer official approval and significance upon school-based curriculum development. But they play, or appear to play, a subordinate role in order to highlight respect for the specialist knowledge residing in the postholders, and an emergent sense of their extended professionalism.

But he points out that far from abdicating leadership responsibilities, his heads exercised these by controlling the direction of change in their schools.

What Campbell describes, as he says, is more of an ideal type than a reality at present. In practice, there are many barriers to primary schools operating in the spirit of collegiality that emanate from the traditional role of the classroom teacher; of a teacher defining his or her responsibilities as the identification and satisfaction of the learning needs of a particular group of children in the school. It is a role generated and maintained by traditional child-centredness, with its implication that the class teacher alone knows enough about his or her children to be able to pronounce authoritatively on their educational needs, and by the sense of security that can result from being insulated in a classroom away from the rest of the school. Classroom autonomy – despite its erosion by influences inside and outside schools – remains a powerful article of faith and emblem of professionalism among primary teachers. Campbell's barriers to collegiality have traditional teacher authority very much at their base. They concern the hazard to personal and professional satisfaction caused by involving teachers in collaborative planning outside their own classrooms and the added danger of conflict among a staff when teachers are asked to move beyond what they perceive as their proper roles. These difficulties are compounded by teachers' general disinclination to accept any other than the head's authority in school-wide matters.

To many teachers working with increasingly large classes and reducing resources, the practical day-to-day obstacles of lack of time and energy might be more important as barriers to change than academic debates about role and authority demarcation. Certainly, the pressures caused by less time and more demands on their energy predispose many teachers to concentrate on their classrooms as their most immediate concern, and this causes them to challenge changes that seek to redraw traditional boundaries. There are also the more pervasive undermining effects, of lowered moral after the longest period of industrial action that teachers have undertaken and the subsequent imposition of a conditions-of-service policy that is condemned by many for the deficit view of teachers as professionals it appears to entertain. Time is perhaps the crucial ingredient. Campbell realistically distinguishes between other contact time, group time, snatched time and personal time; of the first two – which in theory should be available for meetings and planning – he concludes that there is very little in primary schools. This reinforces the HMIs' criticism in their survey of junior schools that a factor preventing post-holders from carrying out their curriculum-leadership roles was that they had too little time outside their own classes for working with colleagues. In the case of his enquiry schools, post-holders had an average of 37 minutes per week of other contact time, which included several having no time at all.

But some of the recent studies he mentions suggest that collegial relationships are developing tentatively in schools. The pattern suggests that teachers are beginning to accept the dual roles of classroom practitioner and group innovator by distinguishing between areas they consider to be their own responsibility and those that are school policy. According to this distinction, proposed changes to teaching methods and classroom resourcing are more likely to be resisted than the production of curricular guidelines. Expertise, providing it concerns school policy, is accepted on an informal, helping basis.

If collegiality provides a beneficial climate for curricular and organizational change, it could be the necessary situation for implementing equal opportunities. In a sense, nobody on the staff is an expert on equality: personal value positions, within limits acceptable to colleagues, are relative and their reconciliation is brought about by people modifying their viewpoints as a result of discourse and reflection, and then acquiring new expertise, as is the case with more routine innovation. Only when the crucial first stage is completed, when value differences are identified and discussed, and an agreed perspective on equality and how to proceed is recorded in the school's equality statement, will the question of individual responsibilities in the implementation process be able to be addressed. But how do individual members of a school staff become a group and how does the group generate the ethos and momentum needed to bring about successful change?

Group Strategies for Change

There is a considerable literature on group-based innovation. The American organization development (OD) work applied to schools – although to British teachers it might seem preoccupied with roles at the expense of their human occupants – provides a basis for development. In particular, the writings of Schmuck *et al*. (1977, 1985), in their handbook form, are a model of how to generate practical measures from established theory.

Organizational development applied to schools emphasizes the co-ordinated interdependence of staff members. Schmuck *et al*. acknowledge that the measure of freedom individuals have in their own classrooms contrasts and often conflicts with the need to collaborate in order to achieve the school's goals, a situation becoming familiar in British schools as the requirement for whole-school policy-making increases. They are concerned with the parts people play in organizations rather than what motivates them as individuals. To apply this focus they distinguish three levels of organizational activity: at the interpersonal level, individuals interact with each other, not necessarily in a goal-directed way. At the subsystem level, working groups within the school go about their business of maintaining certain functions in the school; while at the level of the whole organization, routines and processes continue in their task of maintaining the school as a goal-centred learning environment, in which people and working groups interact and react.

OD works to achieve organizational adaptability, the ultimate goal in a school:

An adaptable organization is continually and consciously solving problems that arise either because groups in the organization's environment are pressing for change or because new goals are being established within the organization itself. Problem solving means reaching out for, remaining open to, and filtering information from both the environment and the organization, examining this information over a period of time, becoming aware of changes that occur, and attempting to predict changes to come. It also means employing systematic procedures to create solutions, changing a normal mode of operation to free resources for new or anticipated problems, and continually rechecking to see whether movement towards goals improves.

(Schmuck *et al.*, 1977, p. 10)

This is very like the Open University school-based INSET course P536's 'thinking' school. Responsiveness to influences inside and outside the school is the main quality aimed for; lack of responsiveness can result from endless discussion, intentional inertia and insensitivity to pressure groups outside, which combine to produce staff fragmentation and therefore an inability to co-ordinate a response. A key feature is the need to disseminate information within the school in order that informed decisions are made by those with particular interests and responsibilities – students, parents, counsellors, teachers, the principal.

The adaptable school is concerned primarily with formulating clear goals, solving problems and making and implementing decisions; and secondarily with improving communications at the three levels and especially between work groups.

In contrast to the behavioural-objectives conception that played a dominant role in curricular design and development in the 1960s and 1970s, goals are multi-dimensional: in Schmuck *et al*'s view, they should describe a new situation to be attained, acknowledge the group's shared values, guide actions intended to achieve them and be able to motivate and sustain the commitment needed to achieve the goal. Behavioural objectives have the single-dimension task of stating what the outcome would be in measurable terms, but goals are more descriptive in the way they include contextual factors:

> Statements of goals are, first, descriptions: they specify a distant state of affairs that is in some way different from the present condition. Second, the goal condition is seen as being better or more attractive to the group according to some set of shared values. Third, goal setting implies the presence of a standard of comparison for judging whether actions carry a group forward or away from the goal. Finally, stating a goal carries an implication of motivated commitment to bring the goal condition into existence.
>
> (Schmuck *et al.*, 1977, p. 147)

For example, these goals were used to revise an elementary school's internal organization:

1. Having the total staff develop, understand, and agree to a philosophy of education that was compatible with individual goals for this school and that included consensual agreements about school policies on various matters
2. Developing clear communication networks, openness, and trust within and across teams
3. Facilitating constructive openness and helpfulness among staff members.

(*Ibid.* p. 162)

The emphasis on goals is heavier than one would find in equivalent British documents, considerably so compared with P536. But it is not a restrictive view: affective factors in goal formation are crucial and must be taken into account, otherwise goals that are unacceptable to some members will be substituted for alternative, private goals meant to divert or subvert the official ones:

> The OD consultant must recognize that goals arise from values, that values differ among people, and that the attractiveness of a goal to group members and the extent to which they will support it will depend upon the extent to which it accords with their own values. This is not to say that the organization is obligated to promote the personal values of all its members but only to suggest that it will find it impossible to achieve its goals if few members derive little personal satisfaction from the effort.
>
> (Schmuck *et al.*, 1977, p. 150)

The use of an outside consultant working with the staff group to formulate and achieve goals is assumed by Schmuck *et al.* but will be a less familiar approach in British schools; however, local-authority advisory and consultant teachers play a similar role to that of the American consultant in reviewing and developing the curriculum, resources and teaching methods. The OD consultant's task includes asking staff members what they think should not happen, as well as what the goals are, and what changes they should be directed to. Furthermore, they are not the perogative of staff: students, parents and other concerned members of the community should also know what they are. In a truly self-renewing school, in Schmuck *et al.*'s terms, personal-needs satisfaction and the efficient exercise of professional expertise and responsibility are two sides of the same coin.

Problem-solving is the means by which the staff achieve their goals. It is a continuous activity, since life in organizations is inevitably beset with conflicts over resources, roles and responsibilities and the exercise of power. A problem is defined by Schmuck *et al.* as 'any discrepancy between an actual state of affairs (situation) and some ideal state to be achieved (target)'. Planning, imagination and anticipation are combined as the work group generates a sequence from identifying, analysing, proposing solutions, designing plans, to forecasting consequences of intended actions, taking action and evaluating the results.

The logical outcome of problem-solving is decision-making; Schmuck *et al.* have found it necessary to efficient working to distinguish between these in practice so that a group is aware of its function and how this resources another group's responsibilities. This idea of a collectivity of groups being responsible for forward planning and day-to-day responsibilities is, of course, very different from traditional top-down decision-making, which is strongly criticized in their rejection of objectives-based management approaches:

> While it is true that subordinates must accept some goal direction if the organiza-
> tion is to carry out its goals effectively, management by objectives is too often just
> another way of increasing pressure on them to produce. Control from the top
> leaves subordinates little room in which to maneuver and virtually no occasion
> for articulating or exploring personal values that might be satisfied within the
> organization. With its single downward direction, it often prevents them from
> expressing ownership of their personal objectives or of experiencing the satisfac-
> tion that comes from sharing in the definition of the organization's larger goals.
>
> (*Ibid.* p. 163)

This view is in conflict with top-down management approaches. Schools are, in Weick's (1970) terms, inherently loosely-coupled systems, in which shared values and working towards consensus in decision-making are in contrast to the very specific role and status allocation and hierarchical arrangements of organizations such as production lines where a top-down approach would be applicable. However, the present government's shift towards a more product-oriented view of education in State schools could lead to a stronger emphasis on top-down management. In contrast, the OD viewpoint implies that power to make decisions is diffused and that decision-making will not follow an orderly line-management kind of progression. It follows also that where people have an amount of power that is consistent with their responsibilities there should be less stress and more job satisfaction, but perhaps more conflicts to be resolved between groups competing for scarce resources. Compared with top-down, rationality is injected into the system: it will be harder for people to be disinterested or unmotivated or only involving themselves in immediate classroom concerns if they are genuinely involved in such decision-making.

In Britain, the recent Open University pack P536, *Making School-Centred INSET Work* (Easen, 1985), is similarly practice-oriented; its core is a series of activities designed to increase teachers' understanding of their own attitudes towards innovation and to equip them with decision-making skills. By acknowledging the importance of teachers' attitudes – the crucial affective dimension of change – it is as 'three-dimensional' as Schmuck *et al.*'s work:

> Any curriculum change has a personal dimension for *each* teacher involved and an
> institutional dimension created by the interactions of *all* those involved. . . .
> Although *curriculum change* may be concerned with the process of identifying,
> defining and resolving problems specific to a particular school, often any real
> change implies:
> • *personal change* as we often need new ways of looking at things if we are really
>   to change what we do; and

● *interpersonal change* to encourage effective communication so that any necessary support can be sought and given during the process of change

(Easen, 1985, p. 8)

Early on it confronts the often problematic issue of teachers' attitudes to
educational theory in a way that accords with the consideration earlier here
of teachers' personal professional ideologies:

> Tucked away in the corners of our professional minds is knowledge which we use
> to help us engage in professional activity with our pupils and with our col-
> leagues. . . . The trouble is that 'tucked away' is often where the knowledge
> stays, unrecognised and therefore not consciously used. The approach of this
> book is based on the belief that, by making explicit the knowledge which is
> implicit, you and your colleagues may generate some ground rules for effective
> school-centred curriculum development.

(Ibid. p. 8)

On the basis of curriculum/personal/professional change, P536 recommends
that each group meeting consists of three stages: of working on the issue
itself, reflecting on the working process and deciding future activity. The
object is to avoid rushing to judgement; of packaged 'solutions' to curricular
'problems' that beset much early large-scale curriculum development based
on the RD and D model, and even the centre-periphery approach adopted
by most Schools Council projects up to the early 1980s. Whatever their
expressed intentions, these emphasized the separateness of the curriculum
expert and the teacher-initiate roles, and the problem of curricular needs
being decided on a system-wide rather than a separate-school basis. As
MacDonald and Walker (1976) show, curriculum development became as
much a selling as a problem-solving exercise, with the most successful
projects, such as 'Geography for the Young School-Leaver' emphasizing
dissemination skills in their team members as an integral part of the
innovation process. Stenhouse, through his radical Humanities Curriculum
Project in the 1960s and 1970s was probably the first curriculum developer to
perceive the essential interdependence of curricular change and teacher
development. The implication – that teachers should become curriculum
researchers in their own classrooms – has become the bedrock principle of
school-based development. While, ten years ago, this might have been
problematic for teachers in technical terms concerning methodology and
role, there were few if any political implications. But with the rise of
accountability, the traditional privacy of teachers' decision-making is increasingly challenged. Since there is increasing pressure from various interested parties for schools and teachers to take direct responsibility for the
outcomes of their decisions, quality control becomes important.

It is not surprising, therefore, that P536 places so much emphasis on the reflective aspects of the practical business of change such as personal theory-building, reflecting on the change processes the group is undergoing and analysing personal constructs. The approach at times has an almost Goffman-like concern for personal and public role-play, at other times is psychoanalytical in style. The picture is of committed, somewhat introspective teachers sensitive to their own and to others' professional needs and potential, aware of the dangers of confrontation but willing to face up to conflict; of teachers as clear-cut individuals, but who define their responsibilities in terms of what is most important to the group. Structure, control and progression as a function of combined personal endeavour rather than hierarchical organization is very much the message. There is nothing about headteachers or other senior staff who, in other models, would have been the expected leaders of change. Leadership, in fact, is seen as an unhelpful, outmoded concept, since the group's need will be to organize themselves rather than be led by someone. This agrees with the concept of chairperson-head in the collegial school.

In summary, both perspectives share much; in particular, how they see the individual teacher's involvement as a group member in making decisions and in their strong advocacy for an interdependent group-approach to decisions. Schmuck *et al.*, perhaps surprisingly – given the traditional classroom autonomy of the British compared with the American teacher – attack the authoritarian nature and inefficiency of top-down management much more directly than does P536. It is as if the British approach is still working through the implications of group problem-solving – school principals as resource providers and change facilitators rather than traditional, from-the-front leaders; of relating, collaborating and communicating with parents, other professionals and interested community members, which American approaches dealt with ten years ago. On the question of goals, Schmuck *et al.* have also arrived at an effective *modus operandi*, probably as a result of the dominance of behavioural objectives as the corner-stone of 'rational curriculum planning' in American education into the 1960s and the ensuing debate and reaction against them. In P536, goals are not mentioned; instead, there are 'resolutions', which are consensus positions arrived at by the innovating group. This is consistent with the process ideology of British education, as the primacy of goals in Schmuck *et al.* characterizes the American product emphasis. Arguably, the P536 approach also mirrors the scepticism about stating educational outcomes in advance, which is involved in the view that curriculum planning should begin with formulating behavioural objectives. It is significant that only one large-scale curriculum project, Schools Council Science 5–13 (1972), has ever used a full-blooded objectives approach. Unlike the USA, the debate about the appropriateness of educational goals has never taken place in Britain because it was pre-empted by the reaction through the whole educational strata against the use of behavioural objectives at least in curriculum planning. This time lapse can also be seen in the development of American-type, performance-objectives-based teacher accountability schemes by local authorities such as Solihull in the late 1970s when this approach was being discredited in the USA.

But in P536 the tension between teachers' classroom and group-innovator roles is acknowledged by the importance the materials attach to teachers' personal motivation and the need for recorded self-reflection as a basis for successful change. What is asserted is the necessary connection between teachers' classroom decision-making and the personal rationales that inform it. The connection remains elusive in spite of much research: the 1970s Ford T Project sought through observation techniques to formulate general principles that would apply to teaching; Hargreaves (1979) advocated a phenomenological approach by which the personal theorizing that under-pins decision-making might be identified, again in an attempt to discover general principles. In America, Eisner (1983) has re-evoked the notion of teaching as an art which Stenhouse's (1975) teacher as curriculum researcher goes some way towards conceptualizing. Each stresses its individualistic nature. The focus is important, since – in a highly-practical sense – what becomes innovation is what is actually implemented in individual class-rooms.

All of this points, paradoxically in view of the group approach to innova-tion arguments offered, towards the upholding of classroom autonomy that in Britain is reinforced by child-centredness. By placing 'the child' at the centre of the educational process, child-centredness emphasizes the role of the classroom teacher as definer and resourcer of children's learning needs before anything else. It is not surprising, therefore, that the concept of teacher as curriculum leader developed in the HMI primary survey and the DES white paper, *Teaching Quality* (1983), is located in and defined by the classroom-teacher role.

It is argued here that equal opportunities will best be implemented through teachers bringing their individual talents, skills, experience and insights to bear on the values and practice issues involved through operating as a collegial group. These qualities themselves will result in individual variations in classroom practices simply because teachers will translate them somewhat differently in their choice of learning resources, materials and topics depending on how they define their children's learning requirements. The crucial aim is to achieve cohesion and development on a school-wide basis through collective action that also allows the exercise of individual judgement at the classroom level. The school-based model presented in the next chapter seeks to keep these two complementary aspects of innovation in view.

6
EQUALITY POLICY-MAKING:
A SCHOOL-BASED
INNOVATION MODEL

The three-stage innovation model presented here depends on several conditions being fulfilled for its successful implementation. The three examples of innovation selected, from different levels of educational decision-making, highlight these. The model is located in a socially-oriented view of child-centredness; it depends on teachers working together in a collegial setting in the policy-formation process; and it takes successful innovation to be the translation of an agreed policy by individual teachers making their own professional judgements within the policy's parameters.

Innovation Processes: Three Examples

The three examples have been chosen to illustrate the processes by which workable equality policies can be developed as a preliminary to the model for innovation that is proposed here. Each is selected from a different level in the educational strata: they are ILEA's anti-sexist policy guidelines for school use; Taylor's paper (1987), also on anti-sexism, provides an adviser's viewpoint; while Milman's (1984) is a primary head's account of implementing a multicultural policy in a school.

There is much that they share. The crucial importance of staff, teaching and ancillary, examining their own attitudes and beliefs privately and within the innovating group as the major precondition for change is emphasized.

The stages by which a policy is formulated will be very much in terms of an on-going appraisal of attitudes accompanied by action. ILEA's guidelines have a three-stage approach, which begins by identifying sexism in the school as a condition for bringing about change and planning a programme of action. About half the suggested questions for discussion by teaching staff concern the position of women teachers in the school: actual and proposed responsibilities allocation, support for career development, position as role models and extent of mutual respect between women and men teachers. Taylor emphasizes the need to identify staff who are well informed about gender issues so that with local-authority support they can inform their colleagues. All three examples advocate using outside consultants or involving other schools that have operative policies. Milman began a series of staff meetings for appraising attitudes and invited a number of people with recognized expertise and authority in the field to participate.

The examples emphasize that reflection is necessary, not in itself, but as a motive force for action. It serves two purposes, both focused on practice: first, to consider and ascertain personal-value positions; and, second, in order to apply these in the school and classroom. The moral impetus within any attempt to increase equality is essentially practical, as has been argued. Two of the examples suggest that teachers be encouraged to conduct small-scale action research-type projects so that they find out more about the processes influencing relationships, decision-making and learning styles operating in their classrooms. Consciously investigating for oneself how one's class functions is not only self-informing as to the processes but is also likely to provoke larger questions about the nature of prejudiced acts – perhaps the way they seem to be unremarkable to children as part of the routine. Taylor (1987, p. 143) comments: 'Then a period of time will be needed for everyone to become better informed and more aware of the evidence of discrimination in their own school. It is a common reaction for teachers to acknowledge evidence from other schools but deny that it is relevant to their own'. She cites Rudduck and May's research as demonstrating how teachers' attitudes can be affected by first-hand evidence. ILEA's document includes a simple classroom observation schedule by which teachers can observe each other at work. The planned observations focus on teaching/learning exchanges and relationships, for instance, how boys' and girls' names are used, how questioning is conducted, the pattern of replies and gender-related remarks made by pupils and the teacher. It also suggests other research topics such as the use of the playground or other public spaces and the use of classroom space for investigations. Taylor also suggests that teachers conduct small research studies in classrooms and share their findings with colleagues. This emphasis on teacher research highlights a concern for exposing the workings of the hidden curriculum both in class-rooms and in the more public areas of the school. It is a recognition of its influence on what children actually come to learn in school over and above the planned curriculum. Clarricoates' (1980) research, for example, is a clear demonstration of how the hidden curriculum shapes behaviour and performance in terms of sex membership by communicating particular learning and behavioural expectations to boys and girls. Milman's approach as a newly-appointed head was not so much geared to individual research as to creating a team spirit based on shared attitudes within a framework of clearly-stated responsibilities.

The three examples agree on the point that formal policy formation should only be embarked upon at a stage when the staff are well informed, committed and actually operating with the policy. It then serves as an expression of confirmed intent and provides a long-term strategy. It is also the means by which the school, parents and governing body can come to terms with each other – though, again, all three stress the importance of liaison and consultation at an earlier stage. In a practical sense, then, having a written-down policy both legitimizes what the staff are already doing and commits the school in the long term. ILEA's guidelines recommend such policy-making because the exercise of committing the policy to print enables greater understanding of the issues, ensures its relevance to the school's particular position and is a public statement to the community outside. Taylor sees the policy as essentially a planning document, while Milman's took the composite form of an aims statement on multi-ethnic education, a job description for the multi-ethnic post-holder and a policy on racism together with his own statement and introduction as head teacher.

They also all emphasize the staff group as the innovating unit. Taylor's recommendations see the policy as a goal-directed planning enterprise incorporating regular reviews of curricular guidelines, and ILEA's guide states the need for immediate and long-term aims and action time-scales, perhaps initially drafted by a working party. Milman, as a new head appointed to a formally-organized school, decided early on that the ethos this generated was too authoritarian for successful multi-ethnic policy-making, and he decided on a collegial approach:

> As a staff we started to take joint decisions about almost everything from discipline to how we should allocate our resources. We viewed curriculum development as a whole school concern and were involved in a continuous process of evaluating where we were and which major initiatives we wished to tackle next. None of this was as easy or painless as it sounds but it was generally wel-comed. . . . Gradually, on an individual basis or in staff meetings, people began to come forward with their concerns. Clearly there was a range of these about multi-ethnic education, including the lack of it. Clearly there was no school policy

on racism and there was a growing demand from the staff that we should do something about it.

(Milman, 1984, p. 35)

Another area of agreement between the three concerns the need for evaluation and review. ILEA's guidelines are strongly behaviour and performance oriented, relying on pupils' reports and teachers' reported observations. Similarly, Taylor's approach is a matter of evaluating outcomes in the form of changes in behaviour, attitudes, skills and knowledge according to the objectives. Her comments (Taylor, 1987, p. 144) balance what is qualitative and quantitative in evaluating:

> It is unrealistic to expect too much change too fast, because the side effects of gender role acquisition in terms of narrowing of individual development are so well embedded in all of us. However, increases in knowledge about what women can do, or have done, changes in expectation of girls' strength, improved use of cooperative discussion techniques from boys, fewer interruptions, fairer use of questioning and allocation of praise, can all be measured.

Milman had no formal procedures but relied on a staff-consultation process and his own overview as head.

Other areas of agreement include the need to involve ancillary workers from an early stage and, as in the emphasis on teachers' classroom research, the influences of the hidden curriculum. In ILEA's guidelines, ancillaries are seen to be very much alongside teachers as concerned staff members. Taylor makes the point that sexist behaviour on the part of non-teaching staff can cancel out positive actions in classrooms, hence the need for their early involvement. Milman (1984, p. 222) saw considerable resourcing potential in his ancillaries:

> We needed to open up channels of communication with our ancillaries; we needed to cash in on their knowledge and experience and to get our messages over to them. We also felt that, traditionally, their status was low in the school. They had to feel that their opinions and feelings were valued.

They therefore had the same access to information to daily events as the teachers and a regular consultation period was developed between them, the deputy head and the head. This is also the procedure adopted by the Ennersdale head. As to the hidden curriculum, ILEA's guidelines seem more concerned with it as the main source of sexism than they are with the actual curriculum; not surprisingly, since the strategy adopted is concerned with personal and institutional sexism as the determining factor in what children come to learn. Taylor (1987, pp. 137–8) also stresses its influence and demonstrates by example how some of its effects can be countered by making its covert assumptions overt through the actual curriculum:

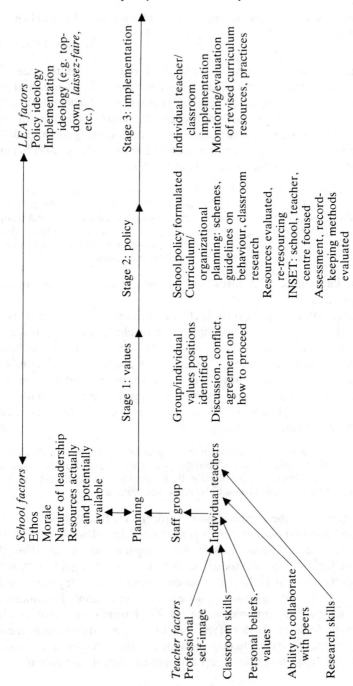

Figure 6.1   Equal-opportunities policy-making: a model for school-based innovation

One teacher of ten year olds asked a girl to move a milk crate. A boy said the girl was not strong enough. The teacher then organised a milk crate lifting competition, and the girls' team managed more lifts than the boys' team, while individual scores within the team varied greatly. It effectively demonstrated two central points: that there are great differences of strength within a sex, and that most girls' and boys' performances overlap. But the boys in the class were most reluctant to accept the very clear evidence, so deep was their engrained belief that boys are stronger.

Milman is also centrally concerned with attitudes and their influence on the hidden curriculum, as his determination to work collegially indicates. His policy formation stems from this tapping the sources of behaviour, with curricula and resources reviews developing the process. One example concerns the development of the infant and junior libraries. For example, a school policy on racism and sexism in books was devised and then used to assess and restock the libraries.

A School-Based Innovation Model

The model proposed here incorporates all of the aspects agreed upon by these three approaches as being important to equal-opportunities policy-making. It could be applied by a school working within the framework of a local-authority policy, or working as an independent institution. The process is in three stages, which overlap in practice: in the first, individual value positions are identified along with the inter-group and personal conflicts they are likely to raise, with the goal of achieving a working level of reconciliation, allowing preliminary planning. The second is concerned with producing an agreed working policy or statement. The third stage involves the policy's implementation, through whole-school curricular guidelines translated in individual classrooms, and reinforced by a formative evaluation strategy for review and renewal purposes (see Figure 6.1).

Although the stages might suggest an ordered, logical process, it is clear from the preceding examples and the powerful affective factors at work that they will overlap and develop unevenly. This particularly concerns the first stage, though by the third it should be possible to think more in terms of action plans with target dates – for example, for reviewing and resourcing curriculum areas. But for the purposes of analysis and explanation each stage will be discussed separately.

Stage 1: Values Debates

The importance of adopting a Milman-type collegial approach that emphasizes co-operation and mutual professional respect is well expressed in P536 (Easen, 1985, p. 16):

Coercion and manipulation are inappropriate in this whole area of curriculum review and development. When we coerce someone we usually know for certain that we are in the right, and therefore ignore the ideas or views that the other person may have. After all, these are either irrelevant or strategies for delay! In order to do this, however, we need to have a suitably large 'stick' which is recognised as such by the victim. On the other hand, manipulation still sees the other person's views as a nuisance. However, instead of ignoring them we subvert them by twisting their ideas to our own purpose. This may well imply some sort of 'carrot'. Neither 'sticks' nor 'carrots' are relevant to this approach.

Pace and work-relatedness are important here. That is, there needs to be preliminary discussion that provides the opportunity for people to speak their minds, with the assumption that individual viewpoints are more likely to be developed through actually doing something practical in the early stages of implementing the policy than through discussion alone – hence the emphasis on teachers' classroom research as a self-informing basis for preliminary action in the examples discussed. A real danger is that the urgency of the issues as perceived and expressed by concerned staff members will swamp other teachers' capacities to take them on board. This stage cannot be seen in purely rational terms as the interaction of minds engaged in debate, as has been argued; strongly-held personal viewpoints often made inaccessible by their rarely being articulated but that are the mainsprings of individual professional practice suggest that the amount of time, pace and quality of debate and conflict management by the staff group will be crucial to successful policy formation. If too much time is devoted to it, the opportunities for conflict and the development of cliques could be consider-able enough to frustrate the whole process. If it was too little, the policy might be a paper policy only with no more than lip service being paid to it by staff who are resentful about their own views being brushed aside as being irrelevant or obstructing.

Whatever P536 says about the primacy of the staff group, this is an appropriate time for the head to exercise overt leadership. When issues confronting personal values are concerned, leadership exercised by a peer, even when he or she is respected by the others, and the leadership is seen to be delegated, can be resented and rejected. Heads are legally responsible for decision-making in their schools. They can initiate potentially-contentious policies with a degree of formal authority a teacher colleague cannot claim, and this at least formally distances heads from dissension among staff members. A cynic or a doubter on the staff might be more disposed to seeing the head as trying to act, misguidedly or otherwise, in the best interests of his or her school, whereas a peer's activities could eagerly be interpreted and rejected as being motivated by ambition. More negatively of course, the head could be seen as going through the motions as required in responding to a local-authority directive, or even trying to protect the staff from unwelcome changes by a boundary-maintaining exercise.

Taylor suggests that staff should be prepared by an oblique process of self-informing: mention of instances of sex-stereotyping in the school in conversation, staff on courses reporting back, followed by small-scale classroom research studies and then the policy formation. Milman's consultation process allied to discussion and review developed people's awareness of the need for a formal policy. It is suggested here that the head – possibly with the deputy – produce a short position paper for the staff to consider, after some preliminary informal consultation and discussion, partly to identify individual attitudes, partly to prepare the way for such a paper. It should not be developed to the extent that it is seen as *un fait accompli*. The first part should be a report analysis of the school, focusing on the composition of the intake, recorded achievement and including some accessible research findings on the educational performance and attitudes effects of class, race and gender-group membership on primary-school children and some of their classroom and school implications. It would be appropriate to their respective responsibilities if copies were circulated to teaching staff, and with the support staff meeting the head for a verbal report and preliminary discussion, with copies available for distribution. The second part would outline the local authority's stance on equal opportunities, even or perhaps especially if it has no policy.

None of this should come as a complete surprise or shock to teachers since it would reiterate in a concrete form what they already know. It would need to be circulated in reasonable time for staff to assimilate it, with a meeting to discuss it being notified in advance. Since it is crucial that everyone attends, it could be held in directed hours as part of the INSET programme, as the Kent policy recommends. The question of who comprises the initial group meeting would need to be decided: the whole staff, with teachers and ancillaries, or a number of separate meetings? If the staff group meet, the point that equal opportunities apply to the whole school and are not only a classroom matter would be emphasized, but the likely disparity of the group could amplify conflict. The internal 'class structure' of the school, in its formal sense of ascribed roles and status, and concerning relationships between co-workers, will be a deciding point. Bringing the two groups together can be traumatic for many but necessary – unless they collaborate a policy cannot be fully implemented.

A carefully-worded statement, then, that defines the area for policy making will not be made in a vacuum. Depending upon the degree of accord between a head and his or her staff, the statement will acknowledge some members' critical view of and dissatisfaction with what the school is presently doing for children who are unequal. As argued earlier, it is also likely to meet with emotional responses ranging from apathy to antagonism. Conflict is inevitable, and necessary to the change process, since too high a level of agreement can insulate the innovating group, even from the intended beneficiaries of the reforms. Milman comments that he and his teachers were taken aback by a critical reaction by the school governers to a report on an early aspect of the school's multi-ethnic initiative, because the school group had become so absorbed in its policy-making activities. 'Groupthink' can dominate; Janis, mentioned by Easen (1985), coined the term to account for the way group conformity can influence decision-making. It describes a group mentality state of rectitude that persuades members into risk-taking; dissidents are neutralized by belittlement and coersion. In this rather paranoid climate, which rests on an assumed unanimity, reflecting on decisions can be seen as attacks upon the group's moral authority; 'mind-guards', or group members who take on responsibility for protecting the group's bogus cohesion see to it that its decisions are based only on information that reinforces concensus. Groupthink can be a product of charismatic leadership, or encouraged by a school staff's resistance to outside pressures – for example, if the local-authority stance is unacceptable to a majority of staff, including the head teacher.

But negative conflict operating at a personal level when the staff group is fragmented by cliques can also prevent policy development. Attacks on colleague's self-images and self-confidence quickly undermine the group's cohesion as mutual trust dissolves or existing differences widen. Miles's (1964) concept of organizational health suggests that certain minimum conditions must apply if any form of innovation is to succeed in a school, and these bear upon morale, institutional self-confidence and mutual professional respect.

Stage 2: Formulating a Policy

The evidence from case-studies of equal-opportunities innovation in schools suggests that policies should not be put into print until there is a high degree of staff support for them. From the point when the policy 'goes public' and governors and parents are involved, the school is committed. The form is also important: there is a considerable difference between a statement of intent, which might be not much more than an expanded version of the head's introductory paper described in stage 1, and a developed action plan with stated goals and time scales. The policy document is the innovatory fulcrum; at the same time, it is the most difficult stage in the sequence to negotiate, and the most important. Judging from past practice, there seem to be two main approaches. First, a statement that explains the school's stance and incorporates a code of practice for all staff and pupils. For example, an anti-racist statement would include a justification for this approach based on the existence of personal and institutional racism and racialism backed up by a code of practice on name calling, racist attacks and stereotyping. Resources and books containing material judged to be racist would be replaced. The curricular and teaching provisions for language would be reviewed concerning mother-tongue maintenance, bilingualism, dialects and English as a second language. Second, a statement and code of practice would provide the basis for a goal-directed action plan with full curriculum, resources, assessment and record-keeping coverage.

The first approach establishes the school's orientation but is limited in its innovation scope. But it could be justified as the first stage in a two-stage process, since its main concern is with attitudes and their behavioural projections; also, resources and language are the foundations for the rest of the curriculum. In a local authority with a developed scheme of curricular guidelines and whole-school policies, recasting these in anti-racist terms could provide the necessary second stage. But if the school is in an authority where such policy-making is embryonic, it will be necessary for it to devise its own plans if the whole curriculum is to be reviewed. In this situation it would be easy to stop at the point of language and resources review, and rely on a permeation process resulting from the code of practice for further development. The problem with permeation by itself is that it is subject to different interpretations and emphases by teachers and is therefore likely to be uneven and incomplete.

The second, more arduous, approach does ensure complete coverage, including the statement and code of practice. It also makes clear what is required by way of curriculum review and renewal from each member of staff in his or her own classroom without necessarily laying down a line of development that spells uniformity. Taylor (1987) suggests that goals should be divided between short-term organizational changes such as alphabetical registers, and medium- and long-term changes concerned with developing learning resources, analysing books and other reading materials, and reviewing the curriculum. If this is founded on a code of practice, the first tasks will be relatively manageable and uncontroversial, paving the way for the more demanding and problematic work. The staff will need to decide how goal-oriented the policy will be. The discussion of goals earlier suggested that they have an insecure position in British education because of its rejection of behavioural objectives. Hoyle (1986) has coined the term 'organizational pathos' to describe the inherent gap between the goals a school formulates for itself and those society ascribes to it. One of the major causes of 'pathos' is that goals emphasize rationality and rely on the rational responses of staff for their achievement; in this they depict an ideal rather than a real world:

> This rationalistic ideal of organisational process assumes the establishment of a clear set of achievable goals, the total commitment of organisational members to these goals, the availability of all the necessary resources, the capacity of organisational members to coordinate their activities, and the unequivocal achievement of successful outcomes. In this direction lies neuroticism, if one takes neurotics to be people who are preoccupied with the discrepancy between an ideal world they carry around in their heads and the imperfect world of everyday experience.

(Ibid. p. 51)

The staff has to confront the goals issue – what will serve its purposes best? How specific should they be, to provide clear but not restrictive directions and to provide a basis for evaluation? Are they even going to be called 'goals'? Three approaches will be suggested here: a check-list system, P536's resolutions and a conventional goal-based scheme. Each can claim to be goal- or at least end-results-directed and each has its advantages and disadvantages in practice. They are probably best used eclectically in combination.

The check-list approach is attractive because it immediately engages staff in the practical problem-solving activity of deciding criteria for applying to behaviour, resources, books and curriculum areas to see whether or not they satisfy equal-opportunities requirements. If the staff group has established a code of practice, this in itself is a check-list since it details what will count as acceptable and unacceptable behaviour on the part of staff and pupils. The example below from Rosendale Junior School's *Multicultural Policy Statement* illustrates the point:

1. Name-calling.
   (a) Encourage individual children to use their full names where possible (especially if the name is unusual or the child appears ashamed of it).
   (b) Staff should ensure they pronounce and spell children's names correctly.
   (c) Literature to be read to classes which includes names from many ethnic origins. Children may then naturally come to respect and accept names from different cultures.
   (d) Teachers to take extra care to explain the correct meaning when using vocabulary which incorporates black images (e.g., black magic) and to decide if it is a necessary phrase. Frequently children misinterpret such words and develop the idea that black is evil, no good, etc.
   (e) Positive teaching about the importance of the origins, meanings of names. Naming ceremonies could be introduced through assembly themes.
   (f) Acknowledgement by all staff that racist name-calling is different from ordinary name-calling, i.e., not just about a child's individuality, but involving insults directed towards a whole ethnic group.

(g) Teachers should take immediate actions when racist incidents occur. A recognition of the need for discussion with other staff who need to gain a full picture of the incident should be developed.

(ILEA, 1982, p. 23)

Check-lists can be devised for all areas of the curriculum, learning resources and books. The example below is from Childeric School's paper on *Assessing Children's Books*:

C. Sex-role stereotypes.
Sex-role socialisation is an important learning experience for the young child.

1. Guard against traditional masculine and feminine roles – the primary feminine role is housekeeping, while the primary masculine role is wage earning.
2. Research has shown that females are under-represented in the titles, central roles, pictures and stories found in children's books. Where there are female characters they are usually insignificant or inconspicuous.
3. In the story, the boys tend to be active and the girls passive. The boys seem to have more exciting and adventuresome roles, and demand more independence. In books, girls are more likely to be seen in indoor situations which place a limitation on their activities and potential adventures, as does their clothing.

(*Ibid.* p. 4)

The approach draws well upon individual expertise and lends itself to small working groups reporting back to the whole-staff-group type of organization. It also provides an effective basis for evaluating progress since the check-list items have a qualitative value in terms of children's learning experiences. A main problem is that the check-lists can assume a life of their own as expressions of working group's viewpoints unless they are devised according to a rationale and terms of reference provided by a clearly-worded, agreed statement as policy position.

Another approach, which, if used in conjunction with check-lists would temper the over-rationality of a goal-directed scheme, is the P536 course's of agreeing resolutions as a basis for decision-making. It differs from goal direction in that it begins with a statement of the problem to be solved rather than with a goal. Then, ideas for resolving the problem are considered; one is selected that seems best to satisfy the various requirements; it in turn is examined for flaws and deficiencies and if it passes this test it is implemented. As with check-lists, this strategy is problem-centred, with teachers analysing and evaluating alternative solutions to curricular and organizational problems. It is best used when something specific and practical has to be decided. The example P536 uses is deciding on a record-keeping method. The first step is to list the available options, then to consider these against the attributes most looked for. In order to organize this, it is suggested that a matrix is drawn up, with the options listed on the left-hand side, and the desired attributes grouped at the top from left to right. Each option is then considered against the attributes using a 1–5 rating system, so that a visible, systematic appraisal develops.

It is important to define this approach as one suited to making decisions about the curricular or organizational framework rather than being a planning strategy: it is usable for deciding which is most suitable among a number of existing alternatives. For example, if a school was developing a locality approach to environmental studies, check-lists could be used to identify the most important learning experiences and most appropriate resources and so forth, while a resolution-deciding approach could be used to consider how children's achievements should be best assessed and the most suitable form of record-keeping for this. The qualitative, prior, question of what would actually count as achievement, perhaps with the Thomas Report's (1985) four aspects of achievement in mind, would be defined in terms of the school's equality statement, particularly if it was based on goals.

No single approach is sufficient in itself. Using goals is the most traditional planning strategy; OD specialists such as Schmuck *et al.* assume that it is the only way. It is certainly the most rational approach – too rational, according to Hoyle. He, and others such as Schmuck *et al.* claim that although institutions like schools are naturally goal oriented, most teachers are unskilled in stating goals. Hoyle suggests that school goals are both diverse and diffuse: diverse because of the wide range of tasks schools try to carry out in the attempt to educate children, and diffuse because they try to bring about essentially-moral changes in pupils that go beyond the instructional. This tends to result in open-ended and unachievable goals being formulated. But he does acknowledge that goals do not have to be geared to specific learning outcomes to be usable in a school; if they are broadly stated, virtually as principles guiding practice, they can be interpreted by teachers who make the final decisions as to how they can be used to serve their children's best interests. The major problem with this is that gaps might appear between the stated goals as guides to action and what teachers actually do in their classrooms. So the dilemma with goals is that unless they are specific and precisely worded they cannot provide the kinds of directions Hoyle and others require of them, but when they are specific and precise they can also be rigid and mechanistic in operation. Perhaps their main obstacle in teachers' eyes is their abstract nature and consequent distancing effect: they seem to presuppose a formality of procedure and practice that is at variance with the informal, face-to-face decision-making in most primary-school staffrooms. They are not 'about' being immersed in the practical business of identifying and solving problems in the way that check-lists and resolutions approaches are. Their main value in equality policy-making might be in designing a general plan for establishing directions and phases of implementation. They can be an effective means of confronting the initial question, 'What are we trying to do?' Taylor's points about having short-, medium- and long-term goals are relevant here. The procedure might be that once the equality statement and code of practice are formed, the head or a small working group might devise a goal-based draft action-plan using these three phases, but with only the short-term goals specified. This would be brought to the staff to consider. The modified results would provide the action plan for the short term; the head, or a working group could then draft the medium-term goals in the same way, then the long term.

Several schools have used statements of aims to define the principles and direction of their equality policies. For example, Annandale School's anti-racist policy combines a statement of general longer-term aims followed by more specific and shorter-term ones under the headings of 'Racism', 'Staff Responses', 'The Curriculum', 'Parents and Resources'. The general aims provide the rationale from which the more specific aims – which amount to being goals in the provision of guidelines sense – are derived. The result is a cohesive, action-oriented code of practice for the whole school that is translatable in individual classrooms according to teachers' judgements. The Rosendale Junior School's multicultural policy lists five general aims all directed towards areas of practice in the school: 'Name-calling', 'Stereotyping', 'Staffing', 'Language and dialect', 'Community'. There is a list of guidelines that amount to operational goals under each heading.

So the three approaches can be used in combination: goals, with aims, to establish directions, phases and time scales, check-lists for review and renewal, and resolutions to decide on organizational features. Together they provide a policy-planning matrix that can be adapted for individual situations and planning tasks. The point is to be eclectic – to use a range of methods in order to plan rather than adhere to one method. Which to emphasize depends on how the task is defined. For example, a staff might decide that goal-setting be limited to establishing directions and general terms of reference in order to become clearer at the beginning about the nature and scope of the exercise. They then might employ a check-list approach for curricular and resources review, with the various areas delegated, and retain their original assessment and record-keeping framework.

Stage 3: Implementation

Questions as to how to implement the policy will already have been addressed, if not settled. The review carried out using the check-lists will have provided the basis for revising the existing schemes according to the agreed policy, or for writing new schemes. The experience will probably not be new, since most schools have undergone collaborative planning-exercises involving all or a majority of the staff, whether in response to local-authority guidelines or planning a school-wide topic for a term. The point, of course, is to ensure as far as possible that the policy is implemented within each class so that the principle of equality pervades all of the teaching and learning in the school. Schemes need to provide clear directions without being strait-jackets: it is important that individual teachers have enough autonomy to be able to interpret and modify what is written down according to how they perceive their children's learning needs. Mutual trust is necessary in a community of interdependent professionals. Mutual trust is also about power sharing; coersion or manipulation are about superior force being exerted to make someone comply. Such measures are essentially reduction-ist in their effects – teachers so used tend to do the accepted minimum in order to pass scrutiny rather than bring their professional skills, experience and insights to bear in the creative business of developing a policy.

It is also important to devise an effective evaluation approach for the short-term, day-to-day operation and the longer-term goals or directions. Here, little will be gained by way of useful diagnostic information if the strategy is imposed, in the form of inspections, for example, or if it only operates summatively, at the end of each year. Evaluation, therefore, needs to be a state of mind in the school. It should include quantifiable information such as achievement levels but it should also gather information about children's behaviour inside and outside classrooms.

P536 suggests that a combination of classroom observations, visits to other classrooms and schools and the use of external expertise provide useful evaluative information. The Open University *Curriculum in Action* materials could be used to equip teachers with classroom participant observation skills that are likely to be the main source of evaluation information, and the P536 guidebook itself has a detailed but easy-to-follow scheme for teachers to base their observations on. ILEA's anti-sexist policy-implementation guidelines advocates analysing pupils' reports to evaluate teachers' expectations and assessment of pupils' achievements, and is a way of obtaining qualitative material on the teaching/learning processes at work in the school. Visiting other classrooms, in the same or a different school, can provide fresh insights by revealing new models or different approaches to familiar ones.

Implementation, like the policies themselves, will always have to be planned in terms of the individual school. The experience of having their policy designated as a good model of practice caused the Ennersdale staff to turn down requests for visits after they saw that some earlier visitors wanted an off-the-shelf solution for their own policy-making problems. They were interested in Ennersdale's policy but not in the processes undergone to produce it and that all schools have to undergo on their own terms. Teachers might be tempted to use what they see as useful package solutions to problems in their own school. Using Hoyle's terms, the organ-transplant approach is likely to end in tissue rejection. Schools are only superficially similar to each other, and to transfer an innovation from the ecosystem in which it was developed to a foreign one is to invite disappointment. But external expertise and experience in the form of teachers operating success-ful equality policies or consultants from the local-authority advisory staff can fulfil a number of supporting roles: running workshops or meetings or working alongside teachers. They are an effective way of building in an evaluative strand in the development of the policy; in an unthreatening sense, they stand outside the staff group and can contribute viewpoints that might not normally emerge in the group's shared understanding.

Conclusions

The process described here has been divided into three separate stages mainly for analytical purposes. In operation, the stages will merge and overlap, as teachers appraise their personal beliefs and value systems, come to terms in various ways with their colleagues, engage with them in planning a policy and implementing and sustaining it. Some of the material concerned with policy-making might seem unnecessarily complicated and even bureaucratic with its emphasis on strategies, documents and meetings. Several points need stressing: each school staff needs to formulate its own line of approach; the whole process cannot be hastened because it is founded on personal and professional reflection as a basis for action. A collegial approach is not as tidy-minded as an external initiative top-down one and will need considerable negotiation, discussion and trade-offs in the form of accepting slightly-different interpretations of what the policy 'means' from one's own – made the more problematic because the group's social climate encourages frankness and explication. Research or evaluation-based teaching with its underpinning of observation by oneself and peers can at first threaten the accustomed privacy of classrooms. But if the policy is to become part of the fabric of learning and teaching in the school, all these factors have to be confronted and answered.

7
A CASE-STUDY OF
EQUAL-OPPORTUNITIES
POLICY-MAKING

A number of approaches to equality policy-making are discussed here, from the school's standpoint as to its role in this; these can be described on a radical-to-moderate continuum as radical-reconstructionist, interventionist, and liberal-educational. The continuum provides a referential framework for the more detailed case-study of Ennersdale Junior School's pioneering race-equality policy, as an example of school-based innovation that was developed before the local authority produced its own statement.

Introduction: a Survey of Approaches

The small number of case-studies published, either in books or circulated in photocopy form by local authorities, have concentrated more on the product – in the form of the actual policies planned – than on the production process, in order to provide examples of successful practice for others. Although the starting points for the examples looked at here are much the same (all but one are concerned with race), the policies reflect the different ways in which school staffs conceptualized the issues and produced responses appropriate to their own circumstances. It is a truism that no two schools are alike, except in features such as the intake age-range, establishment and financing. But it might be assumed that the policies produced would be similar because of what is generally understood of the aetiology of racism and sexism, even though the processes undergone in formulating them would have to be different. Or, considering policy-formation strategies, that the stages as described in the model will be the same so far as development and progression is concerned, but that the ways these are negotiated will differ from school to school. Gaine's (1987) survey of secondary schools' race-equality policy-documents indicates that their starting points were racist incidents and other expressions of racism inside the schools and in the locality. The examples all begin by emphasizing this and defining their major task as combating racism and racialism by modifying pupils' behaviour inside and outside the schools. Only then are the curricular implications of anti-racism addressed. In demonstrating how these schools decided on their priorities, the examples also make more clear the essential differences between the 'negative' combating-racism stance and the 'positive' one of enriching the curriculum multiculturally. While a policy is for the whole staff, it is bound to be more for the uninterested or unconvinced members than the committed, and while Gaine suggests that the curriculum-reconstruction approach rather than anti-racism is likely to attract the first group, he queries its possible effectiveness:

> We must be clear what the issue is. Is it that a richer, broader curriculum awaits us if we only had less ethnocentrist eyes to see it? This is positive, optimistic reasoning, presenting a multicultural approach as an opportunity, not a threat. There are times when it must be sold this way, and if presented like this it may reduce the anxiety and resultant hostility in many teachers. We should not be under any illusions, however, that the world is really such a happy place. If multiracial schools have failed to respond in this way for the past twenty years or more, if they find that even with black children in their classrooms they can only now begin to get policies when these pupils are victims of racist violence, it may be naive to think that a more positive approach will work elsewhere.
>
> (*Ibid.* p. 128)

More generally, the literature of school-based change suggests that apprehension and anticipation in different proportions influence the extent and nature of possible change, according to how far proposals match individual teachers' professional ideologies and draw upon their expertise. In the case of equal-opportunities innovation, the conditions are more problematic for reasons that have been discussed.

All innovations are conditional since they are state-of-the-art expressions: they represent a particular staff's capacity at the time to improve on the status quo in their school. Because of the heavy attitudinal and self-reflection emphasis underpinning equal-opportunities policies, these are even more subject to questioning as more comes to be understood about the conditions they have been planned to meet. Mulvaney, head of an infants' school in Hackney at the time, argues with reference to his school's multicultural policy:

> At best, such a policy can only be a compromise between existing staff views and attitudes. There is much that could be added, and words that should be omitted. The policy is only valid at the time it was written (1980) and for a short time afterwards. Given changes in staff, children and parents, levels of awareness, and the community it should be reviewed and modified annually. Most importantly, a policy should be an affirmation of practice and not an unrealistic list that can never be achieved.
>
> (Cited in Straker-Welds, 1984, p. 29)

He also raises questions as to the school's stance behind its policy statement: does it signpost it as an agency for community action, working on behalf of parents and children by combating the discrimination they experience, or does it have the more-limited educational function as the basis for reviewing learning and teaching? Broadly, equality policies – especially concerning race – can be described as *radical-reconstructionist*, where the school sees its role as actively working for the community of which it is part by involving itself in such issues as housing and the role of the police, or *interventionist*, where the school sees its main task as combating racism and racialism on its own premises and in a limited way in the immediate neighbourhood, or *liberal-educational*, where a cultural diversity set of aims is brought to bear on curriculum regeneration. Mulvaney's school's stance was clearly radical-reconstructionist since it was involved directly with the community through the staff's opposition to the Nationality Bill, their intercession with Hackney Council over its refusal to rehouse a Sikh family, and their decision that the police should not enter the school premises except in an emergency until they had examined their racism and established effective links with the local community. He sees Gayhurst's anti-racist policy as necessarily involving the school in community affairs if it is not to be seen as a racist institution by black parents:

> I suspect that all the anti-racist policies that schools are preparing will have very little effect upon the alienation that the community feels. The possession of a policy and its operation within the school will not have a great impact on the community at large. Unless the school is overtly anti-racist, and taking a principled position on these issues in the community, it will, despite the best intentions, be regarded as racist. Eventually, we must recognize that racism is a black issue that the black community must struggle against and find solutions for. As white middle-class teachers, the best we can do is to examine ourselves, our practice, and support them in that struggle.
>
> (*Ibid.* p. 33)

But other schools would claim that degrees of involvement are possible. Schools that have anti-racist or sexist policies operate these through laid-down procedures for staff to follow in confronting racist or sexist actions or comments. At the very least these indicate for all to see the school's level of concern about racism and sexism. They are a code of practice that extends outside the school's premises to the local community. For example, the following extracts from Redlands School's policy details what counts as expressions of racism, inside and outside the school, and how staff are to deal with them:

EXAMPLES OF RACISM WHICH MAY OCCUR BETWEEN CHILDREN

1. Physical assault against a person or group because of colour or ethnicity
2. Derogatory name-calling, insults or racist jokes
3. Racist graffiti or any other written insult
4. Provocative behaviour such as wearing racist badges or insignia
5. Bringing racist material such as leaflets, comics or magazines into the school
6. Making threats against a person or group because of colour or ethnicity
7. Racist comment in the course of discussions or lessons
8. Attempts to recruit other pupils to racist organisations or groups

STRATEGIES FOR DEALING WITH SPOKEN RACIST INCIDENTS

a. Identify what was said and what it means.
b. Involve the whole class or group and explain that the term used was abusive and designed to hurt.
c. Say that behaviour of this kind is unacceptable.

1. It may be necessary to consider classroom management skills in order to call the attention of the whole school/group to a racist incident. This means the adult must feel relaxed about interrupting a group lesson. All teachers will therefore be encouraged to develop discussion skills so that responses to racist incidents can be assessed to see if the children have understood the language and concepts used.

(Redlands School, *Code of Practice for Anti-Racist Policy*, photocopy, pp. 6–8)

Many statements would end here, but this school extends staff action into the community:

RACIST INCIDENTS WHICH OCCUR OUTSIDE THE SCHOOL

A. Incidents which happen outside school, outside school time.
   Parents will be offered advice and information about support services should they request them.
B. Abuse and attacks which occur when children are coming and going to school, the school will:-
   1. Talk with the children involved, listen to their account and comfort them.
   2. Talk with any witnesses.
   3. Try to acertain specific facts i.e. age, gender, school uniform (if appropriate) time, etc.
   4. If the offender is an adult, the police will be contacted.

5. If the offender is of school age, the teacher will try to identify the school from a description of the school badge/uniform etc.
6. Their school will then be contacted and cooperation will be sought in identifying the children in question.
7. An agreement will then be made as to who will follow up the incident.
8. If we are to follow up the incident, our procedures are to interview the suspected child/ren, listen to his/her account. If the interviewer has grounds to suspect the child/ren, she will inform the offender that racist behaviour is illegal and discuss the possible involvement of the police. The suspected child/rens parents will be informed and invited to participate in discussing further action to ensure the incident is not repeated.

(Ibid. p. 11)

The Redlands approach can be described as interventionist compared with Gayhurst's radical reconstructionism; their stands against racism and racialism are equally clear, unequivocal and practical. Redlands' is a coherent, realizable policy within the school and in certain settings outside it, while Gayhurst's is bound to take the school into larger community-politics issues that it might, or might not, be able to influence. That one stance is politically 'safer' than the other hardly needs debating.

Annandale Primary School's document, referred to earlier, demonstrates the liberal-educational response that concentrates on curriculum and resources review underpinned by an anti-racism standpoint. This is less specific than Redlands as to types of incidents; there is more stress on the need to modify stereotypical thinking and prejudice among children and staff through teaching and learning activities. It is, in this sense, less political than Gayhurst or Redlands, and more educational-practices based in the ways it draws upon the multicultural-education literature. It is set out in goal form; for example, under the heading 'The Curriculum':

(i) To encourage an interest in and understanding of different cultures and societies around the world.
(ii) To teach children that each society has its own values, traditions, customs and belief systems. To show how cultural differences arise from geographic and climatic factors and have a crucial influence on living patterns.
(iii) To teach children to identify stereotypes whether of class, race, gender or handicap, and to be critical of them.
(iv) To examine prejudice from experiences of the children in their own lives and relate these to the wider community.
(v) To support the maintenance and value of bilingualism in general and mother tongue competence, both oral and written.
(vi) To study the political, social and economic reasons for racial inequality.
(vii) To encourage the appreciation of other cultures through their achievements in the Sciences and the Arts.
(viii) To examine the faith and belief systems of other societies and relate them to the moral codes of our society.

(Annandale Primary School policy, photocopy, p. 3)

In contrast, Hanover Primary School's liberal-educational anti-sexism policy developed as a result of a re-evaluation of aspects of the curriculum, resources and organization as part of a long-term plan to formulate whole-school policies on anti-sexism and racism, discipline and for all areas of the curriculum. The first policy established was on disciplinary procedures that reduced the confusion and charges of unfairness brought about by children being dealt with differently by different teachers. The staff's professional attitudes concerning the lack of unanimity were important for the school's subsequent policies, and for all other schools engaged in such policy-making:

> Despite much professional collaboration, dispute and self-examination, we could not achieve total unanimity about all parts of the policy. Nevertheless the staff agreed that as it had been formulated and agreed upon by the majority of staff, even those not wholly in agreement would carry out the policy in full. This decision was to have great significance in all our future work on policy. The commitment by all staff to upholding the majority decision made policies effective in the school.
>
> (ILEA, 1986, p. 7)

Through the re-evaluation exercise they found activities that were sex-differentiated both in availability and performance. For example, in the fourth year, girls' marks in English and mathematics were significantly lower than those of the boys.

As a result of evaluating the resources, many library, reading and picture books were discarded because they contained stereotypes and biases. But the most sex-differentiated areas were in the teaching of football, netball, woodwork, needle-work and recorders; in lining up in, and the use of, the playground; in registers; and in classroom grouping. By this point the need for an anti-sexist policy as a basis for change was recognized and accepted by many of the staff, and the experience of the successful discipline policy provided the impetus and self-confidence for them to begin to plan.

A Case-Study of Policy-Making: Ennersdale Junior School

(I am indebted to Roger Hurn, Deputy Head of Ennersdale Junior School, South East London, and Thames Polytechnic Primary Teacher Fellow for 1987–8, for his collaboration and for the material that comprises this case-study.)

The move towards policy-making was a grass roots one: about 1977 to 1978 it had become clear to the staff that many ethnic-minority families in the neighbourhood were deliberately sending their children to Ennersdale.

It appeared that this was not so much due to particular demographic reasons as to a discriminatory reaction on the part of many white families who were sending their children to other schools – the school down the road, virtually in the same area, was all white. Ennersdale, therefore, was becoming defined as a 'black' school. A number of hitherto underlying concerns increasingly became overt. One reaction on the part of the staff was anger at the apparent racism in the neighbourhood, which was causing this movement. The head of the 'white' school was also disturbed by the causes of the concentration of white families in his school to the extent that he tried to dissuade them from not sending their children to Ennersdale. But the staff's major concern focused on Ennersdale as a learning environment and particularly on its curriculum. The main questions raised were, 'Was it meeting the children's needs?' 'Who defines these, anyway?' There seemed to be a strong sense of events outside threatening to overtake the school and the staff were becoming aware of the possible dangers of their responding reactively to these in an ethnocentric way: that, as a reaction to the changing intake, the staff would make some superficial changes rather than the more radical and proactive one of embarking on a conscious and co-ordinated programme of analysis leading to innovation. So there was a stage when the staff, pressured by the need to review and innovate, were in conflict with one another over the direction innovation should take. One point of conflict was the charge that some teachers were paying lip service to multiculturalism and going through the motions, rather than identifying and recording examples of good practice.

These concerns continued to be debated and as staff members became more familiar with them as a fact of life at Ennersdale, they began to acquire a more positive interpretation. This was summed up in the view that if many ethnic-minority families were happy to send their children to Ennersdale, what was the school providing for them?

This position was the basis for the first policy statement, which was then drawn up. The fact that the staff group itself was multi-ethnic in composition, with black, Turkish and Greek Cypriot members, and included two with a strong involvement in NAME (National Association for Multiracial Education) gave the move initial impetus.

By 1980, 80 per cent of Ennersdale Junior's intake was composed of children from a range of ethnic-minority groups. In January 1980, a new Deputy Head was appointed (Roger Hurn) a year after the appointment of a new Head. At their interviews both candidates had made it clear that they were committed to a multicultural perspective as a basis for development. The staff group briefed this new management team on the work done so far, which was regarded as a central strand of development in the school.

Important groundwork had been established, but there was now the need for a new impetus to be led by the Head and Deputy. This lead would be an acknowledgement of what the grassroots – the staff group – had achieved, in order to make the pattern of teaching and learning in the school more responsive to the children's needs, and to forge further links with parents. In Roger Hurn's words,

> We wanted to make public what we were doing in order to get the ideas across and to explain to parents and outsiders what we meant by multiculturalism and what was happening to our curriculum – how we could value kids from different cultures, and how their contribution was valued by the school.

The school decided to run a multi-ethnic day-conference in the summer of 1980, very much in the spirit of its perceived role as a community school, in order to make its position clearer and to disseminate examples of good practice to a public composed of local-community members and other interested groups and individuals. The then MP, Roland Moyle, was invited to open it. The format consisted of, first, a public meeting in one of the halls with a panel of prominent experts from the field to introduce it, followed by a number of discussion groups led by teachers; second, a mini-carnival opened by a dancer and singer from the Commonwealth Institute with costumes and dancing. The panel members' addresses at the public meeting centred on their views and beliefs about multi-ethnic education, with the emphasis being on communicating a framework of attitudes on which to build multi-ethnic education. Jocelyn Barrow's contribution was representative and well received. It was directed particularly to parents, and stressed the partnership between them and teachers, which she thought essential to a child's acquisition of an education. It was worded in terms of maintaining high expectations in attainment and behaviour, and that a failing child is everybody's concern. Many of the staff, including the new management team, felt that she voiced their long-term concerns, particularly regarding the partnership in learning between parents, children and teachers.

Although the conference had received official commendation, the attendance had been disappointing, after all the staff's efforts, and it was not repeated in spite of Roland Moyle's wish that it would become an annual event. The school, along with others, was entering a period of falling roles due to low birthrates and staff redeployment. With the staff losses and some lowering of morale, the momentum needed to mount another such conference was not regained. Much of the morale problem was due to the expectation that the school would be given support to develop its acknowledged pioneering and outstanding work in developing multi-ethnic education, rather than be told by the authority that it would have to lose staff. But the development of the school's multi-ethnic policy continued, notably through its involvement with a variety of outside projects. In 1982, for example, it was one of six schools participating in the Schools and Museums Project, linked with the Horniman Museum and the Museum of Mankind. The previous year the school mounted a week-long exhibition on China, including a musical, *The Dragon Lord*, based on Chinese legends, and written by the Deputy Head. The exhibition took the form of cross-curricular links developing multiculturalism through drawing on different cultures including those in the local community. Parental and children's involvement was high, as was the attendance, especially for the musical performances.

In 1983 ILEA issued its anti-racism guidelines. Although the school had been pursuing a multicultural, essentially pluralistic approach, some staff had political and educational beliefs that inclined them more towards anti-racism. The experience of several years' development of a multicultural community-based education inevitably brought teachers in confrontation with racism. The school was committed to the promotion of positive self-images among its children, celebrating cultural differences through being involved in and directly drawing upon parents' and others' culture. Teachers also made themselves part of this experience through their willing-ness to share their own culture with the children. That the approach also entailed recognizing and trying to come to terms with the racism that children and their parents experienced was acknowledged. The staff, however, were not unanimous that anti-racism was the definitive approach; the political spectrum represented on the staff included radical black consciousness and black-power perspectives at one end to assimilationism at the other. At the same time the authority's anti-racism approach did not come as a surprise.

The staff's response, therefore, was carefully considered and founded on their extensive experience of developing multi-ethnic education. The teachers welcomed the guidelines as a way of impelling schools to act, as they had done so several years earlier. But there was unease at the way ILEA had launched its initiative: the view was expressed that the authority had defined the problem, and also the solution. In this there seemed to be two related sources of concern and dissent: there was the feeling that the top-down style of implementation ignored what schools such as Ennersdale were already doing through their close relationship with the communities they served, and the view that if school communities were different and had different needs, it is not possible to have one centrally-imposed solution. The staff were happy, therefore, to have the problem defined but contended that they should be responsible for its solution.

So the staff began to develop its policy. The process took 10–12 weeks of 1½- to 2-hour meetings after school when personal views were explained and debated, examples of good practice in the school identified, a programme of evaluation based on participant observation planned and, more generally, standpoints and lines of development established. A useful range of contributions from another perspective was made by an exchange teacher from Chicago; one of the points she made was that while she considered that the USA was twenty years ahead of Britain in work of this kind, she had observed far less overt racism here. She also felt that black children in the school tended to have stronger self-images than many she had taught in America; they felt they were accepted within the Ennersdale community-oriented and child-centred approach, which impressed her. She herself had found the adjustment to child-centredness from a more behaviourist tradition both demanding and rewarding in terms both of teacher–child relationships and the freedom to be more imaginative. She also considered that although it could be made to work by experienced teachers, it was too lacking in external structure for new teachers.

Her view that as a starting point personal racism should be admitted by everyone on the staff provoked disagreement and some derision. The key question in the ensuing debate focused on whether or not such admissions would be productive. The staff by and large eventually rejected it as a formal approach but at the same time members expressed their preparedness to identify and to confront their own prejudices and shortcomings with their colleagues. In fact a considerable amount of meeting time was spent discussing individuals' positions on race. Two examples of the honesty with which this was done will be illustrative here: one teacher, strongly committed to NAME, and a part-time worker in a multiracial youth club, admitted what he perceived to be a prejudice against Nigerians in his inability to get on with them. An Asian teacher declared a strong assimilationist personal position, which he summed up by stating, 'I came to England to eat Lancashire hotpot, not curry!' He felt that multiculturalism should be an issue that concerned parents, in the way they chose to bring up their children, and not part of what the children should experience in school.

The ancillary staff were involved through a series of half-hour meetings per day, which the Head conducted in their rest period. They had been supportive as a group since the multi-ethnic conference in 1980, which many attended. One person refused on personal grounds to endorse the policy because she felt she was being pressured – rather as the teachers had felt on receipt of ILEA's guidelines.

The school was congratulated by the adviser for the quality of its policy; it was one of three taken up as examples for other schools. While it took twelve weeks to produce, it is still being developed and its ramifications worked out.

Part of the Policy

Ennersdale Junior School.
Policy for Education in a Multicultural Society.

We are pleased to be able to present a further response to the Authority on multicultural education in the knowledge that now, all schools have been requested to respond in the same way. The staff see this as a major advance by the Authority and one that should have taken place when earlier statements on multiculturalism were produced.

We still see it to be the case that many people in this country must gain their own cultural identity in order to understand their role in society. It is still the case that education can be a potent force for well-being between races and developing a child's full potential will be a useful tool in developing identity. At the same time identity will further enhance that success. We feel that helping children to succeed will help them to identify; and to identify will also help us to succeed.

This re-statement of our basic philosophy echoes much of this report and our earlier report. The structure that the rest of this report will follow is similar to our previous report but will re-iterate, emphasise, up-date and change in the light of our experience.

a) *The Social Setting of the School.*

Despite a further fall in roll our school composition has changed little in the last few years. Our children still largely come from working class families and have a wide variety of racial background. The problems of good housing, play space, and general Inner Urban deprivation still exist.

b) *The Ethnic Composition of our School.*

At present about 53% of our children come from ethnic minority groups. Our school is enriched with children from such diverse cultural backgrounds as: Jamaica, Barbados, Trinidad, Guyana, Nigeria, Ireland, Cyprus (Turkish), Fiji and China. We have just one respected member of our staff, Mr R. Gupta who comes from an ethnic minority group.

c) *Teacher Attitudes.*

It is one of the most important priorities of the staff to develop the ethnic consciousness of the school. It is our belief that to treat all children alike when their needs are so different is incorrect. The individual needs of the child are paramount and this remains at the core of our thinking thereby enabling us to provide equality of opportunity for all.

1. Teachers are necessarily caught up in the process of transmitting social and cultural values. We are not, and indeed never really have been a monoethnic

society. We are a racially mixed society and we must start our educational thinking from this fact.

2. We are pleased to see a good advance in multi-ethnic education in both initial and in-service training.

We are pleased to see that special courses have been arranged with the specific intention of increasing the number of black people entering teacher education. We believe that appointments made by the Authority at all levels are crucial to the whole question of multi-ethnic education and believe that a candidate's knowledge of this field of education should be given a high priority when recruitment takes place.

3. Our aims for the school are to show to our parents and children that we happily accept the idea of cultural pluralism. We must show that we accept this fact by giving equal validity and significance, by all we do and say in the school, to cultures other than our own. Children are very quick to perceive teacher attitudes and we are all extremely aware of the fact that our own attitudes may be the most pervasive and significant element in promoting racial harmony within school.

4. *How Teacher Attitudes Affect School Life.*
(modification of the curriculum)
The corollory of positive teacher attitudes towards multi-cultural education is that they wish to revise not only what is taught, but also the materials which are used for teaching.
Curriculum We believe that there are two factors to consider:
a) *Specific teaching* – related to other cultures i.e. their history, geography, music, literature, art, etc.
b) *Implicit teaching* against racial attitudes by extending whatever is being taught to include a 'world view' of subjects and ideas and not merely presenting a single-sided view of life.

Both of these aspects are important to multi-ethnic education, but we believe that it is important to stress the fact that multi-ethnic education does not begin and end with a map of the West Indies pinned to the wall.

Multi-ethnic education may well begin with recognising and valuing the culture which the child brings to school, and building upon this for the education of all our children. For example in mathematics we give wide and valued credit where other cultures have contributed to our knowledge of the subject. Some instances are: – the many and varied number systems developed by cultures other than the British; the contributions made by the Egyptians and Greeks to systems of mensuration; the geometrical ideas implicit in such things as the design of the North American Indian or in Rangooli patterns; and the extremely competent way in which the Chinese developed the use of the abacus.

5. *Materials.*

Children learn best when building upon those things which they already know. There needs to be recognisable elements within the environment which offer the security from which to venture further.
That is why we have paid particular attention to our choice of materials in the Junior School. We are a multi-racial society and we believe that it is necessary therefore to have materials in our school which reflect this fact. The presence of a

multi-ethnic content has been a major consideration when selecting books for the school and class libraries, and also when selecting books to be used for the teaching of reading.

The staff of the Junior School do not believe that the teaching of reading is a *neutral activity* and that the material used, therefore, is inconsequential, and that the child may make his own choice of material once the skill has been acquired. As teachers we understand that what is being read must have meaning and significance for the child, and that material which undermines and undervalues that which has deep meaning for the child may act as a direct barrier to learning. Since we view our job as being to remove as many of the barriers re learning as possible, the presentation of appropriate material is of great concern to us.

6. The whole question of language is a complex one. There is a delicate balance that exists where the child needs to learn standard English whilst at the same time not devaluing the child's home language. The school does not have the facilities to teach languages other than English; the staff are pleased to see the Authority initiatives in supporting groups that can help bi-lingual children. Where the child's first language is not English learning the child's home language can be of great benefit. We welcome, therefore, the Authority's initiative so that groups that cater for the parents' wishes in this area, like those at the Lee Centre, can exist and flourish.

7. *Reactions to Rampton.*

Our previous multi-ethnic report followed Mr Newsam's papers and since then we have considered a major report, 'West Indian Children in Our Schools' under the chairmanship of Anthony Rampton. This lengthy report gives eighty recommendations, some of which we feel we are pursuing. The emphasis placed on multi-ethnic education throughout the service was a very important one and can only enhance the work going on as it will no longer be doing it in isolation.

8. *Parents.*

We feel that parental involvement is a key issue in our school. We keep an open door policy and parents are welcome to see staff virtually at any time. Apart from our formal occasions such as open evenings we are trying to get as many home/school links as possible. This is one reason why staff have been keenly involved in 'Friends of Ennersdale'. We still believe mutual trust between staff and parents to be of the utmost importance.

9. *Conclusion.*

We believe that the presence of ethnic minority group children positively enriches our school, and we totally disassociate ourselves from the view which says that their very presence constitutes a problem. We all need to learn from each other and we believe that school is the best place to take advantage of such opportunities.

Ways in which the special educational needs of children are met.

Children with special educational needs are usually identified by the teaching staff. Their needs can vary greatly; some require extra help because for various reasons they have slipped behind in part of their academic development or conversely children of above average ability requiring a group situation where they can be stretched, encouraged and further develop individual abilities. Under normal circumstances these children can be helped within the school situation.

(1983)

Discussion

The policy is liberal-educational with interventionist elements. A notable feature is its concern with conceptual learning: it is a framework of concepts, skills and attitudes that the staff identify as being their children's learning and development needs. Since it is not content-specific but is a referential system for selecting content and learning experiences, it provides a context rather than a blue-print for curriculum renewal serving all the children in the school. This is very much in the spirit of *Education for All*, which it predated by two years; implicit is the claim that children's learning needs are universalistic, that different approaches might be justified because of different learning growth-points, and that teachers are in a unique position to identify these. The principles do not change but the content by which they are represented might be different in different schools and at different times as the policy is developed. It is a quality shared with many of the school policies mentioned here; it characterizes a child-centred approach with the strong recognition of the social contexts within which the children grow and develop. It also recognizes that having high achievement aspirations and making real demands on children is also universalistic – it is not the perogative of white, middle-class intake schools in the suburbs.

What is also vital in supporting this approach is that the staff provide good role models – the Ennersdale staff's willingness to share the implications of their own ethnic diversity with the children is characteristic. In this way the school is emphasized as a learning institution.

All of these factors stress the importance of the process by which a statement is produced. Because the Ennersdale statement was commended by the authority as a model, there were many requests for it from other schools developing their own policies. In some cases they wanted the statement off-the-shelf, with little consultation sought and no regard for the processes involved in producing it. The Ennersdale staff eventually discouraged further requests because they saw consultation of this kind as being a waste of time for all concerned. What is crucial then is the non-transferability of such statements: they can be models in terms of providing referential frameworks for other schools to compare their own ideas with, and they identify the concerns that should be central to all statements. But each school has to arrive at its own position on its own terms. The innovation model developed in the previous chapter rightly stresses the importance of this process and the commitment to a policy position it generates. As Roger Hurn puts it, the school's educational principles and practices become multicultural, rather than 'multicultural education' being bolted on to what already exists, such as posting a map of the West Indies on the wall for a week or two.

But staff unanimity on such complex and demanding personal and professional issues is unlikely to be there at the outset, and open to suspicion if it is claimed to be. The Ennersdale staff were in agreement, with some exceptions and reservations, with the anti-racism/multicultural basis of the policy, and were not unanimous on how it should be implemented. There was a balance between taking collective responsibility for the principles and retaining individual autonomy in implementing these throughout the school and in classrooms. This position underlines the school-based nature of equality policy-making. A key both to Ennersdale's perceived position as a community school and to its multicultural principles is the central importance to its staff of children developing a positive identity and self-concept. What Ennersdale stresses is the universal importance of having a positive self-concept, which gives all the children the confidence to succeed in school. This connects with the earlier point about the universality of parents' achievement aspirations, which the staff have been aware of for a long time through parents' involvement with the school. As Roger Hurn points out, it sometimes comes as a surprise to teachers in schools in more favoured areas, that black working-class parents can have high aspirations for their children.

It might seem surprising that a more overt anti-racism stance was not adopted, considering the strength of the staff's commitment and also the nature of ILEA's policy. Certainly, racism is recognized and confronted in its behavioural forms as the case-study and the policy document show. Because of the school's long history as a community school in an impoverished neighbourhood, together with the trust that parents placed in it, the staff felt it unnecessary to make more of their anti-racism, which they considered was well understood. Developing the well-established multicultural base was the school's solution.

8
CONCLUSION: THE FUTURE OF EQUALITY?

What can schools and teachers do to foster equality within the enterprise culture? In the period since ILEA's equality policies were published, the climate for egalitarian reform has deteriorated as the opposing forces have become more polarized with the advance of central control and the redistribution of power between the DES, local authorities and the schools. Some indicators include Berkshire, a pioneering local authority, that has sought to revoke its anti-racism policy after only five years' operation. Its multicultural education sub-committee planned to replace it with the more limited strategy of combating under-achievement among Afro-Caribbean children, but the policy has been reinstated following protests from concerned groups. The Dewsbury parents have been allowed to send their children to the mainly-white Overthorpe School rather than the 85 per cent Asian-intake Headfield School, mostly due to a flaw in the education committee's admissions policy (*The Observer*, 17 July 1988). This decision could provide a precedent for white parents who wish their children to go to predominantly-white intake schools, as the local MP, Ann Taylor, has pointed out. It could become a more common practice, since under the Education Act, schools themselves will largely be in control of their own intake numbers. More significant for the future of local-authority race-equality initiatives, the media reportage of the murder of an Asian pupil at Burnage High School has provoked a backlash against anti-racist policies, though what was at issue was not the policy but the manner of its implementation, as the committee of enquiry made clear.

The Education Act overshadows such indicators, however. The amount of central control initially envisaged has grown with its passage through both Houses with the extra clauses and amendments that have been added. According to Jack Straw, the Labour education spokesperson, the Secretary of Education's new powers have increased from 175 to 415, which includes 49 acquired as the bill made its way through the House of Lords (*Guardian*, 18 July 1988). A major change that affects the form of development of multicultural education is the Lords' amendment that religious education and daily assemblies shall be 'wholly or mainly' Christian, with the provision that children of other religions will have the right to their own assemblies. Moreover, there seems to be little or no room for an anti-racist, or anti-sexist or multicultural, interpretation of the Swann kind of the core and foundation subjects in the national curriculum. The National Convention of Black Teachers is reported (*The Times Educational Supplement*, 26 February 1988) as being concerned about the Act's provisions for two reasons: it claims that no recognizable and representative minority group had been consulted at any point when the curriculum proposals were being formulated, and that the proposals do not include any consideration of race factors. It points out, for instance, that the proposed monitoring tests seem to take little or no account of the extent of language diversity in the school population and its implications. Their points amount to a fear that the national-curriculum subjects, together with benchmark testing, will be planned in ethnocentric 'white-culture' terms. Other interested groups have publicized their views; considering the present political balance of power and the reforming nature of the Act, the situation favours those on the political right getting the larger audience.

For example, the Centre for Policy Studies' pamphlet, *Correct Core* (reviewed in *The Times Educational Supplement*, 25 March 1988), argues for a 'minimilist' core curriculum of English, mathematics and science aimed at producing literacy, numeracy and a basic scientific understanding by school-leaving age. It rejects child-centred methods and emphasizes a transmission view of teaching and learning. This extends to its view of required educational knowledge, judging, for example, by its performance targets in English. While these emphasize generally-accepted qualities such as fluency, legibility and precision, the learning material list stipulates the Authorized version of the Bible, Shakespeare, Milton, Pope, Wordsworth, Keats and Tennyson.

But the curriculum proposals have the potential for promoting gender if not race equality, since they entail that all pupils in State schools will have access to the same educational content between 5 and 16. This represents a formal condition, a basic, flat-equality situation. There is some evidence from other European countries such as France, Denmark and Sweden that suggests that when boys and girls have a common educational experience and common attainment targets up to about 15 years, some equalizing of life chances can occur: Byrne (1985) suggests that in these countries a significantly larger proportion of girls are now entering traditionally male-dominated work, further education and training. Of course, this is not necessarily due to the effects of schooling alone. What characterizes these and other countries such as the Netherlands is that their education systems are based on sex-equality policies that seek to ensure that every boy and girl achieves a minimum level of competence in all the compulsory subjects. In Britain, the reduction of subject options at 14 and the inclusion of science as a core subject ensures increased rather than equal access, but the new order should go some way to bringing about the closer links between attaining school knowledge and having higher-status careers, which Deem (1978), argues as being a means to increasing sex equality. It would be naïve, however, to expect that access alone will result in increased equality of achievement, in the absence of an articulated sex-equality policy operating within the curriculum proposals. Levels of awareness and the ways pupils continue to be grouped and taught are likely to remain important determinants of achievement.

The situation highlights the crucial importance of the benchmark tests as a potential means of monitoring equal achievement, if there is the political will to do this. For the first time in State education there will be detailed age-related national records of achievement that could be used for more far-reaching social-justice ends than those of measuring gains in the system as a whole or comparing the schools for efficiency. Potentially, the tests could yield unprecedented amounts of detailed information on the performance of all children throughout their schooling. The figures could be used to combat the negative beliefs, still widely held, about the behaviour and achievement potential of black children as an undifferentiated group. They could also be used more selectively as a justification for better ESL and mother-tongue teaching. Girls' performance figures in the traditional male-dominated areas of the national curriculum could be used in the same ways. For race, a central policy for developing such monitoring has already been outlined in the Swann Report's recommendations under the heading of suggestions to those in authority, leaving aside its proposals for a multicultural curriculum. Gender, because it presents fewer problems to official-dom, politicians and the public, has not been the subject of central government policy-making to anything like the same degree as race. Arnot's study (1987) of central-government policy responses to sex equality evidences this uninterest, and it suggests that a considerable shift in official opinion would be needed for this to change.

As to primary schools, and especially the junior age-range, the core subjects English and mathematics represent in the form of basic-skills teaching and learning what research studies such as ORACLE suggest is the bulk of primary teaching and learning, with an estimated two-thirds of school time being devoted to them. If this is so, they already fulfil a major part of the central-curriculum directives. But the addition of science to the core represents a considerable potential levelling-up in favour of girls' learning.

These points suggest that the efficiency ethic behind the national-curriculum directives is likely to produce some spin-off results favouring the promotion of educational equality. It is unlikely that any government of whatever political colour would launch a reform programme with much else than raising performance in order to produce more efficiency as the goal, given the public-funding basis of State education. This can be seen in terms of a possible sequence of priorities, depending on the political persuasion of particular administrations, in which the primary goal might be to make the system more efficient; the next most important might be the less concrete meritocratic one of increasing individual life-chances through raised educational performance, or equality of opportunity; and, at a distance, the most abstract goal of promoting race and gender equality. A potentially more negative effect of government action involves both the new conditions of service and the drive towards efficiency and teacher accountability. Together they could influence the direction of equality policy-making in schools in two ways. First, parents and governors could raise questions as to whether the school's main priority should be the more pressing and tangible one of raising achievement standards, or the more abstract one of increasing equality. The onus would be on the professionals in the school to demonstrate that the two can be connected. Second, given the increased power of parents and governing bodies, teachers' authority to lead the implementation of problematic and controversial measures such as anti-racism and sexism policies might be questioned. Stenhouse's point (1975) about the necessary rectitude of schools is applicable here. The possibility of schools opting out of local-authority control is a further complicating factor. The climate for operating radical-seeming policies has also not been improved by the abolition of the most prominent of the left-wing authorities, which also had a well-publicized equality policy.

At the same time and more positively, local authorities across the political spectrum continue to produce policies, Kent's being one of the most recent. If about half the authorities in England have equality policies operating it at least means that a large number of teachers have had varying amounts of exposure to the equality principle and its educational applications.

What should schools attempt? It was suggested earlier that intervening in the teaching/learning process to raise achievement levels of disadvantaged groups and individuals might represent a realistic target given the amount of power schools and local authorities have. Deem (1978) argues that efforts to reduce inequalities in schools provides examples for others by raising awareness elsewhere as to the possibility of change. Inside schools, of course, more straightforward goals may be more immediate; teachers may wish to promote equality because they are challenged by unfairness and unrealized potential. But should they proceed on a general front, as proposed for instance by the Kent policy, in which achievement equality in general is promoted by modifying learning processes, grouping and materials, or should their goals have a specific focus, such as combating racism or sexism? Gaine (1987, p. 179) warns against the notion of prejudice being substituted for racism, in particular, as a cause of inequality, and the sidetracking effect this has on teacher action:

> It seems to lead inexorably towards a psychological view: if prejudice is so pervasive and directed against so many groups by so many groups, it must be a basic feature of human beings, it must be Human Nature. Whether it is or not, it is plain that it is going to be with us for a little while yet, and precisely because it is so broad and all embracing, I would argue, from practice in classrooms, that it is impossible to work against it as a generalised phenomenon.

The more general problem of equating anti-prejudice with pro-equality confirms his practical point. As prejudice is a psychological phenomenon it is confined to group and individual attitudes and behaviour to others, and is taken to have no structural/institutional basis: it is not possible to claim that the law or the education system is prejudiced, only that some lawyers and teachers are. It is possible to claim that some individuals are made unequal by the way they are treated by the law or the education system through its procedures, and that they are also subjected to prejudiced behaviour. Therefore it is, at the least, difficult to try to achieve goals concerned with promoting equality only by attacking prejudice, and not perceiving the structural, institutional nature of inequality. This kind of approach might deal in a general way with 'what' but hardly at all with 'why'. For example, it might be possible to make white children more tolerant of some Asian groups' food preferences by having a class topic that investigates how certain herbs and spices are used by some people rather than others, and getting them and Asian children to prepare and to sample foods in a horizon-broadening exercise. But how far is it possible in this way to make children understand why different groups eat different foods? If the explanations are in terms of the availability of certain ingredients in parts of India, or the suitability of the diet to the climate, this invites the rejoinder that, since they are now in Britain, why do they not eat British food – Lancashire hotpot rather than curry? The problem with teachers seeing prejudice as the root of all evil is its tangibility as a motivator: it simply is more 'there' in classrooms as an explanation of unacceptable behaviour compared with the more abstract and remote nature of inequality connected with racism or sexism. As a cultural-harmony approach, it is also safer than one promoting race equality. Rather than food, a teacher would have to embark on potentially more-contentious topics such as the extension of the franchise or colonial expansion, although investigating the history of sugar production might be a suitable food topic.

But there are also dangers in being too specific. While prejudice is a powerful motivator, just because it is unfair and therefore wrong, a concentration on one area of inequality such as racism or sexism could be seen by those staff members who have reservations about it as more an assertion of special ideological interests rather than promoting equality. This could have the detrimental effect of the policy being seen to be for the oppressed group only and not having the interests of all children in mind, and of the staff being divided over the whole question of where the priority should lie. It has been argued here that teachers need to be clear in themselves as to how they understand the concept of equality and the range of its implications in practice, and that equality policies stem from this initial analysis. When these analyses are brought to bear collectively on the school's situation it begins to be possible to formulate a workable policy. It might be that a school staff decides that its initial priority is race, but it would be difficult to see them being able to relegate other areas of inequality for very long. There are too many connections between class, race and gender inequalities – not to mention the somewhat different area of inequality due to disabilities – for a staff to consider one to the exclusion of the others. It was no accident that ILEA's policy was entitled *Race, Sex and Class*. The cultural projections in terms of sex inequalities in some racially-mixed schools cannot be ignored:

> Boys from ethnic minorities can succeed relatively well in schools, especially if they have families who are ambitious on their behalf. Such families, however, usually have no such ambition for girls, and the presence in a lesson of boys of their own community can be the most painful and oppressive aspect of it. For such girls, I would argue, there is no space for relaxation, and even the most relaxed parts of the school day (eg lunch hour) are potentially, if not actually, tense and tortuous.
>
> (Amara, 1984, p. 6)

Likewise, there are dangers for teachers who are less knowledgeable than they need to be about the topics they choose with the intention of combating sexist stereotypes:

For example, many teachers have decided to study famous women in 'herstory'. Such programmes often include Elizabeth I, Elizabeth Fry, Madame Curie, Sylvia Pankhurst and Amy Johnson. But educationalists cannot continue to study individuals in isolation from the political/social framework of their era. How can Queen Elizabeth I continue to be described as a glorious monarch (many teachers still do this) when during her reign the English peasantry suffered oppression and starvation, when John Hawkins began the Atlantic slave trade, when Sir Francis Drake plunged England into a long history of plunder and exploitation, when Black people in England were being deported and when the rights of English women stood in stark contrast to those that held the power? Elizabeth I was indeed a 'great leader' for some of her people, for some of the time but to ask critical questions of the Elizabethan age is to move in the direction of an anti-racist/sexist herstory.

(Davis, 1985, pp. 15–16)

Her further point is that often white middle-class women are extolled as image-breakers, and to ask why these in particular are so visible. Her argument suggests that it is misleading to consider figures like the explorer, Mary Kingsley, for instance, exclusively in terms of their female assertiveness ignoring other questions such as their class membership, knowledge and relationship with men and women in different classes, political beliefs and activities, and their views on sexism, racism and imperialism.

Gaine's argument (1987), that racism should have a higher priority in schools because it is worse than sexism, will be both unconvincing and unacceptable to many teachers because of the interconnectedness of class, race and sex factors in equality, which is very clear once its structural nature is accepted. That racism is more prominent and has led to violence and that sexism is more pervasive and therefore more likely to be taken as natural is not a strong argument for putting race first. On these terms, it could be argued that combating sexism is more important because it affects more people. Indeed, in all-white schools – rightly or wrongly – sexism rather than racism is likely to be more immediate and problematic to many teachers because of the way it affects girls' access to learning and achievement, with racism being a rather remote social phenomenon outside most staff's and children's experiences. Of course, the counter-argument to this is that it is precisely in all-white schools that the fact of a multiracial Britain needs to be brought home, but this will not necessarily be self-evident.

There are also the bedrock set of issues concerning social-class membership and inequality that focus on the links between definitions of educability and working-class under-achievement in terms of these. In some views, race membership is subsumed in class membership, with another version of the cultural-deprivation explanation being used to account for low achievement. The problem of class and school achievement will be more familiar to many teachers than those concerning race or gender because they will have encountered it in their initial teacher–education courses. Such factors as language usage, attitudes to authority figures, motivation and long-term aspirations are less likely to be the subject of equality policies than identifying more routinely some values and practices issues to do with learning in schools with a largely working-class intake.

Another group experiencing unequal treatment not discussed here in terms of equality policy-making are those pupils with special educational needs. They are subject to prejudice and discrimination in much the same way as race groups. But as Gaine points out, the position of the disabled concerning structural inequality is in contrast with that of women and ethnic-minority group members, although their legal position is similar. For example, 'Unless one conceives of the able-bodied as an oppressor group, it is difficult to see the notion of able-bodied as having been developed to maintain and justify a set of power relations, where one group benefits from the oppression of the other' (Gaine, 1987, p. 181). He also points out that disability can mean just that: it is real in a way that race and gender is not, because having a particular disability actually can prevent someone from doing a particular job – as he says, there are no wheelchair-bound police or blind electricians. But if these kinds of self-evident physical prohibitions are set aside, the issue of equal opportunities still applies, and beyond it the question of structural equality: how far can someone whose disabilities mean that there are grounds for special educational treatment expect to be able to compete on equal terms with the non-disabled in the British education system and beyond it? At the practical level, the inequality in provisions in local authorities means that some children will never be defined as having special needs, while others will both be defined and have their needs met in separate schools, or units attached to mainstream schools, or they will be integrated fully into the mainstream. At the level of values, the connections between having a disability and being made unequal focus on the process of being designated 'special'. Bash *et al.* (1985, p. 110) claim that the diagnosis is essentially socially constructed and provides the justification for segregation:

> The picture is of a smiling 8-year-old Downs' Syndrome child in a bright, well equipped classroom with a competent-looking young teacher adjusting some piece of technological apparatus in the background. The emphasis is on help, and studies of special education have likewise tended to focus on the most efficient methods of helping those unfortunates with special needs: they have appropriately emerged from the disciplines of psychology or even medicine. These traditional perceptions of special education doubtless give one version of the social realities. It is a perception based on the acceptance of dominant ideologies of intelligence, behaviour, normality and individualism.

The particular case of disruptive units and the process of being referred to one based on behaviour that cannot be ameliorated or contained in mainstream schools is both an extreme and a not-uncommon example of socially-constructed diagnosis and segregation.

In this view, children with special needs experience prejudice in the form of stigmatization, which has much the same effects on self-concepts and achievement as has been claimed for race groups and girls. Also, as recipients of special education they are connected to the same processes of social stratification and division of labour. In this kind of analysis, therefore, they stand in the same relationship to equality as do women and ethnic-minority members.

However, their inclusion in local-authority equality policies is low-key after race and gender for a range of reasons concerning resources, diagnosis, provision and politics that is beyond the scope of this book. This will go some way to explaining, and perhaps justifying, why race and gender have been concentrated on here as being the main – but not exclusive – focus of school policies. The question of how teachers might decide their school's priorities and how best to work in their children's interests remains.

REFERENCES AND BIBLIOGRAPHY

Alexander, R. (1984) *Primary Teaching*, Holt, Rinehart & Winston, London.
Amara, N. (1984) 'An alien environment', *Issues in race and education*, no. 41, pp. 5–8.
Arnot, M. (ed.) (1985) *Race and Gender. Equal Opportunities Policies in Education*, Pergamon Press, Oxford.
Arnot, M. (1987) 'Political lip service or radical reform?' in M. Arnot and G. Weiner (eds.) (1987) *Gender and the Politics of Schooling*, Hutchinson Education, London.
Arnot, M. and Weiner, G. (eds.) (1987) *Gender and the Politics of Schooling*, Hutchinson Education, London.
Ashton, P., Kneen, P. and Davies, F. (1975) *The Aims of Primary Education: A Study of Teachers' Opinions*, Macmillan Education, Basingstoke.
Barnes, D. (1976) *From Communication to Curriculum*, Penguin Books, Harmondsworth.
Barnes, J. (1975) 'Curriculum innovation in London's EPA's', *Educational Priority*, Vol. 3, HMSO, London.
Bash, L., Coulby, D. and Jones, C. (1985) *Urban Schooling. Theory and Practice*, Holt, Rinehart & Winston, London.
Bennett, N. (1976) *Teaching Styles and Pupil Progress*, Open Books, London.
Boyd, J. (1984) *Understanding the Primary Curriculum*. Hutchinson Education, Basingstoke.
Bynner, J. (1980) 'Black and white arguments', *Guardian*, 18 March.
Byrne, E. (1978) *Women and Education*, Tavistock, London.
Byrne, E. (1985) 'Equality or equity', in M. Arnot (ed.) *Race and Gender. Equal Opportunities Policies in Education'*. Pergamon Press, Oxford.
Campbell, R. (1985) *Developing the Primary School Curriculum*, Holt, Rinehart & Winston, London.
Carrington, B. and Short, G. (1987) 'Breakthrough to political literacy: political education, antiracist teaching and the primary school', *Journal of Educational Policy*, Vol. 2, no. 1, pp. 1–13.

Cashmore, E. and Troyna, B. (1983) *Introduction to Race Relations*, Routledge & Kegan Paul, London.
Chin, R. (1968) 'Basic strategies and procedures in effecting change', in E. Morphet and O. Ryan (eds.) *Designing Education for the Future*, No. 3, Citation Press, New York, NY.
Clarricoates, K. (1980) 'The importance of being Ernest . . . Emma . . . Tom . . . Jane', in R. Deem (ed.) *Schooling for Women's Work*, Routledge & Kegan Paul, London.
Clarricoates, K. (1983) 'Some aspects of the "hidden" curriculum and interaction in the classroom', *Primary Education Review*, no. 17, summer 1983, pp. 10–11.
Cocking, L. and Craig, D. (eds.) (1984) *Education in a Multiethnic Society. The Primary School.* ILEA.
Cohen, L. and Cohen, A. (eds.) (1986) *Multicultural Education. A Sourcebook for Teachers*, Harper & Row, London.
Cox, C. and Dyson, A. (eds.) (1969) *Fight for Education: a Black Paper*, Critical Quarterly Society, London.
Craig, I. (ed.) (1987) *Primary School Management in Action*, Longman, Harlow.
Crosland, A. (1962) *The Conservative Enemy*, Cape, London.
Dalton, T. (1988) *The Challenge of Curriculum Innovation,* Falmer Press, Lewis.
Danziger, K. (1971) *Socialisation*, Penguin Books, Harmondsworth.
Davis, V. (1985) 'Is your anti-sexist work racist?', *Multi-Ethnic Education Review*, Vol. 4, no. 2, pp. 15–22.
Dearden, R. (1968) *The Philosophy of Primary Education*, Routledge & Kegan Paul, London.
Deem, R. (1978) *Women and Schooling*, Routledge & Kegan Paul, London.
Deem, R. (ed.) (1980) *Schooling for Women's Work*, Routledge & Kegan Paul, London.
DES (1977) *Curriculum 11–16*, HMSO, London.
DES (1978) *Primary Education in England: A Survey by HM Inspectors of Schools*, HMSO, London.
DES (1980) *A Framework for the Curriculum*, HMSO, London.
DES (1981) *The School Curriculum*, HMSO, London.
DES (1983) *Teaching Quality*, HMSO, London.
DES (1985a) *The Curriculum from 5 to 16*, HMSO, London.
DES (1985b) *Education for All* (the Swann Report), HMSO, London.
DES (1987) *The National Curriculum*, Consultative Document, HMSO, London
Driver, G. (1980) *Beyond Underachievement*, Commission for Racial Equality, London.
Easen, P. (1985) P536: *Making School-centred INSET Work*, Open University/ Croom Helm, Beckenham.
Eisner, E. (1983) *Cognition and Curriculum*, Longman, Harlow.
Eysenck, H. (1971) *Race, Intelligence and Education*, Temple Smith, London.
French, J. (1986) 'Gender and the classroom', *New Society*, 7 March, pp. 405–6.
Gaine, C. (1987) *No Problem Here*, Hutchinson Education, London.
Grace, G. (1978) *Teachers, Ideology and Control*, Routledge & Kegan Paul, London.
Green, P. (1982) 'Teachers' influence on the self-concept of ethnic minority pupils', unpublished PhD thesis, University of Durham.

Hargreaves, D. (1979) 'A phenomenological approach to classroom decision-making', in J. Eggleston (ed.) *Teacher Decision-Making in the Classroom*, Routledge & Kegan Paul, London.

Hargreaves, D. (1982) *Improving Secondary Schools*, ILEA, London.

Hebb, D. (1979) cited in M. Hardy and S. Heyes (eds.) *Beginning Psychology*, Weidenfeld & Nicolson, London.

Hirst, P. (1974) *Knowledge and the Curriculum*, Routledge & Kegan Paul, London.

Hoyle, E. (1975) 'The creativity of the school in Britain', in A. Harris, M. Lawn and W. Prescott (eds.) (1975) *Curriculum Innovation*, Croom Helm, Beckenham.

Hoyle, E. (1986) *The Politics of School Management*, Hodder & Stoughton, Sevenoaks.

ILEA (1981) *Education in a Multiethnic Society. An aide-memoire for the inspectorate*, London.

ILEA (1982) *Anti-Racist School Policies*, Multi-Ethnic Education Inspectorate, spring, London.

ILEA (1983a) *Race, Sex and Class. 1. Achievement in Schools*, London.

ILEA (1983b) *Race, Sex and Class. 2. Multi-Ethnic Education in Schools*, London.

ILEA (1983c) *Race, Sex and Class. 3. A Policy for Equality: Race*, London.

ILEA (1983d) *Race, Sex and Class. 4. Anti-Racist Statement and Guidelines*, London.

ILEA (1983e) *Race, Sex and Class. 5. Multi-Ethnic Education in Further, Higher and Community Education*, London.

ILEA (1985a) *Race, Sex and Class. 6. A Policy for Equality: Sex*, London.

ILEA (1985b) *Implementing the ILEA's Anti-Sexist Policy*, London.

ILEA (1986) *Primary Matters. Some Approaches to Equal Opportunities in Primary Schools*, London.

Jayne, E. (1984) *Sex (Gender) Differentiation* (mimeo.), Avery Hill College, London.

Jeffcoate, R. (1984) *Ethnic Minorities and Education*, Harper & Row, London.

Jenkins, Rt. Hon. Roy, Address given by the Home Secretary to a meeting of Voluntary Liaison Committees, London: NCC1.

Jensen, A. (1969) 'How much can we boost I.Q. and scholastic achievement?', *Harvard Educational Review*, Vol. 39, no. 2, spring, pp. 1–123.

Kent County Council Education (1988) *Equal Opportunities in the Curriculum*, Area Education Office, Gravesend.

King, R. (1978) *All Things Bright and Beautiful? A Sociological Study of Infants' Classrooms*, Wiley, Chichester.

Lee, J. (1984) 'Contradictions and constraints in an inner city infant school', in G. Grace (ed.) *Education and the City*, Routledge & Kegan Paul, London.

Lawton, D. (1980) *The Politics of the School Curriculum*, Routledge & Kegan Paul, London.

Little, A. and Willey, R. (1981) *Multi-ethnic Education: The Way Forward*, Schools Council pamphlet 18, London.

Lobban, G. (1978) 'The influence of the school on sex-role stereotyping', in J. Chetwynd and O. Hartnett (eds.) *The Sex Role System*, Routledge & Kegan Paul, London.

MacDonald, B. (1975) 'Innovation and incompetence', cited in L. Stenhouse, *An Introduction to Curriculum Research and Development*, Heinemann Educational, London.

MacDonald, B. and Walker, R. (1976) *Changing the Curriculum*, Open Books, London.

Macoby, E. and Jacklin, C. (1975) *The Psychology of Sex Differences*, Oxford University Press.

Macoby, E. and Jacklin, C. (1980) 'Psychological sex differences', in M. Rutter (ed.) *Scientific Foundations of Developmental Psychiatry*, Heinemann Educational, London.

Meighan, R. (1986) *A Sociology of Educating*, (2nd edn.), Holt, Rinehardt & Winston, London.

Midwinter, E. (1972) *Priority Education*, Penguin Books, Harmondsworth.

Midwinter, E. (1973) *Patterns of Community Education*, Ward Lock Educational, London.

Miles, M. (1964) 'On temporary systems', in M. Miles (ed) (1964) *Innovation in Education*, Teachers College Press, New York, NY.

Miles, M. (1975) 'Planned change and organisational health: figure and ground', in A. Harris, M. Lawn and N. Prescott (eds.) *Curriculum Innovation*, Croom Helm, Beckenham.

Milman, D. (1984) 'Childeric School: developing a multicultural policy', in M. Straker-Welds (ed.) *Education for a Multicultural Society*, Bell & Hyman, London.

Milner, D. (1983) *Children and Race. Ten Years On,* Ward Lock Educational, London.

Mullard, D. (1982) 'Multiracial education in Britain: from assimilation to cultural Pluralism', in J. Tierney (ed.) *Race, Migration and Schooling*, Holt, Rinehart & Winston, London.

Nash, R. (1973) *Classrooms Observed*, Routledge & Kegan Paul, London.

Oakley, A. (1982) *Subject Women*, Fontana, Glasgow.

Parekh, B. (1983) 'Educational opportunity in multi-ethnic Britain', in N. Glazer and K. Young (eds.) *Ethnic Pluralism and Public Policy*, Heinemann Educational, London. Cited in DES (1985b) *Education For All*, HMSO, London.

Peters, R. (ed.) (1969) *Perspectives on Plowden*, Routledge & Kegan Paul, London.

Rendel, M. (1985) 'The winning of the Sex Discrimination Act', in M. Arnot (ed.) *Race and Gender. Equal Opportunities Policies in Education.* Pergamon Press, Oxford.

Rex, J. (1973) *Race. Colonialism and the City*, Routledge & Kegan Paul, London.

Rex, J. and Tomlinson, S. (1979) *Colonial Immigrants in a British City*, Routledge & Kegan Paul, London.

Richards, C. (1982) 'Primary education: 1974–80', in C. Richards (ed.) *New Directions in Primary Education*, Falmer Press, Lewes.

Rosenthal, R. (1973) 'The Pygmalion effect lives', *Psychology Today*, Vol. 7, no. 7, pp. 56–63.

Rubovits, P. and Maehr, M. (1973) 'Pygmalion black and white', *Journal of Personality and Social Psychology*, Vol. 25, no. 2, pp. 210–18.

Rudduck, M. and May, N. (1984) *Sex Stereotyping in the Early Years of Schooling*, University of East Anglia, Norwich.

Runnymeade Research Report (1985) *Education For All*, a summary of the Swann Report, Runnymeade Trust, London.

Rutter, M., Maughan, B., Mortimore, P. and Ousten, J. (1979) *Fifteen Thousand Hours*, Open Books, London.

Schmuck, R., Runkel, P., Arends, J. and Arends, R. (1977) *The Second Handbook of Organization Development in Schools*, Mayfield Publishing Company, Palo Alto, Calif.

Schmuck, R. and Runkel, P. (1985) *The Handbook of Organization Development in Schools* (3rd edn.), Mayfield Publishing Company, Palo Alto, Calif.

Schools Council (1983) *Primary Practice*, Working Paper 75, Evans/Methuen, London.

Schools Council Science 5–13 (1972) *With Objectives in Mind*, MacDonald Educational, London.

Selleck, R. (1972) *English Primary Education and the Progressives, 1914–1939*, Routledge & Kegan Paul, London.

Sharma, S. and Meighan, R. (1980) 'Schooling and sex roles: the case of GCE "O" level mathematics', *British Journal of Sociology of Education*, Vol. 1, no. 2, pp. 193–205.

Sharp, R. and Green, A. (1975) *Education and Social Control*, Routledge & Kegan Paul, London.

Skilbeck, M. (1971), 'Strategies of curriculum change', in J. Walton (ed.) *Curriculum Organisation and Design*, Ward Lock, London.

Skilbeck, M. (1984) *School-Based Curriculum Development*, Harper & Row, London.

Spender, D. (1980) *Man-made Language*, Routledge & Kegan Paul, London.

Stenhouse, L. (1975) *An Introduction to Curriculum Research and Development*, Heinemann Educational, London.

Stone, M. (1981) *The Education of the Black Child in Britain*, Fontana, Glasgow.

Straker-Welds, M. (ed.) (1984) *Education for a Multicultural Society*, Bell & Hyman, London.

Taylor, H. (1987) 'A policy for combating sex stereotypes in the primary school', in I. Craig (ed.) *Primary School Management in Action*, Longman, Harlow.

Thomas, N. (1985) *Improving Primary Schools*, ILEA, London.

Tierney, J. (ed.) (1982) *Race, Migration and Schooling,* Holt, Rinehart & Winston, London.

Warnock, M. (1977) *Schools of Thought*, Faber & Faber, London.

Watts, J. (1988) 'The Power Game', *Guardian*, 24 April, p. 33–4.

Weick, K. (1970) 'Educational organizations as loosely-coupled systems', in *Educational Administration Quarterly*, 21.

White, J. (1975) The end of the compulsory curriculum, in *The Curriculum. The Doris Lee Lectures*, Studies in Education 2, University of London Institute of Education.

Whyte, J. (1983) *Beyond the Wendy House: Sex Role Stereotyping in the Primary School*, Longman, Harlow.

Wicksteed, D. and Hill, M. (1979) 'Is this you? A survey of primary teachers' attitudes to issues raised in the Great Debate', *Education 3–13*, Vol. 7, no. 1, pp. 32–6. Cited in R. Campbell (1985) *Developing the Primary School Curriculum*, Holt, Rinehart of Winston, London.

AUTHOR INDEX

SUBJECT INDEX